James William Sullivan

Direct Legislation by the Citizenship through the Initiative and Referendum

Trough the Initiative and Referendum

James William Sullivan

Direct Legislation by the Citizenship through the Initiative and Referendum
Trough the Initiative and Referendum

ISBN/EAN: 9783744729499

Printed in Europe, USA, Canada, Australia, Japan

Cover: Foto ©Suzi / pixelio.de

More available books at **www.hansebooks.com**

DIRECT LEGISLATION

BY

THE CITIZENSHIP

THROUGH

THE INITIATIVE AND REFERENDUM

BY

J. W. SULLIVAN

CONTENTS:

NEW YORK
TRUE NATIONALIST PUBLISHING COMPANY
1893

AS TO THIS BOOK.

This is the second in a series of sociological works, each a small volume, I have in course of publication. The first, "A Concept of Political Justice," gave in outline the major positions which seem to me logically to accord in practical life with the political principle of equal freedom. In the present work, certain of the positions taken in the first are amplified. In each of the volumes to come, which will be issued as I find time to complete them, similar amplification in the case of other positions will be made. Naturally, the order of publication of the proposed works may be influenced by the general trend in the discussion of public questions.

The small-book plan I have adopted for several reasons. One is, that the writer who embodies his thought on any large subject in a single weighty volume commonly finds difficulty in selling the work or having it read; the price alone restricts its market, and the volume, by its very size, usually repels the ordinary reader. Another, that the radical world, which I especially address, is nowadays assailed with so much printed matter that in it big books have slight show of favor. Another, that the reader of any volume in the series subsequent to the first may on reference to the first ascertain the train of connection and entire scope of the thought I would present. And, finally, that such persons as have been won to the support of the principles taught may interest themselves, and perhaps others, in spreading knowledge of these principles, as developed in the successive works.

On the last-mentioned point, a word. Having during the past decade closely observed, and in some measure shared in, the discussion of advanced sociological thought, I maintain with confidence the principles of equal freedom, not only in their essential truth, but in the leading applications I have made of them. At least, I may trust that, thus far in either work, in coming to my more important conclusions, I have not fallen into error through blind devotion to an " ism " nor halted at faulty judgment because of limited investigation.   I therefore hope to have others join with me, some to work quite in the lines I follow, and some to move at least in the direction of those lines.

The present volume I have prepared with care.   My attention being attracted about eight years ago to the direct legislation of Switzerland, I then set about collecting what notes in regard to that institution I could glean from periodicals and other publications. But at that time very little of value had been printed in English.   Later, as exchange editor of a social reform weekly journal, I gathered such facts bearing on the subject as were passing about in the American newspaper world, and through the magazine indexes for the past twenty years I gained access to whatever pertaining to Switzerland had gone on record in the monthlies and quarterlies ; while at the three larger libraries of New York—the Astor, the Mercantile, and the Columbia College—I found the principal descriptive and historical works on Switzerland.   But from all these sources only a slender stock of information with regard to the influence of the Initiative and Referendum on the later political and economic development of Switzerland was to be obtained.   So, when, three years ago, with inquiry on this point in mind, I spent some months in Switzerland, about all I had at first on which to base investigations was a collection of commonplace or beclouded fact from the newspapers, a few statistics and opinions from an English magazine or two, and some excerpts from volumes by De Laveleye and Freeman which contained chapters treating of Swiss institutions.   Soon after, as a result of my observations in the country, I contributed, under the caption " Republican Switzerland," a series of articles to the New York " Times " on the Swiss government of today, and, last April, an essay to the " Chautauquan " magazine on " The Referendum in Switzerland."   On the form outlined in these articles I have constructed the first three chapters of the present work.   The data, however, excepting in a few cases, are corrected to 1892, and in many respects besides I have profited by the labors of other men in the same field.

The past two years and a half has seen much writing on Swiss institutions. Political investigators are awakening to the fact that in politics and economics the Swiss are doing what has never before been done in the world. In neighborhood, region, and nation, the entire citizenship in each case concerned is in details operating the government. In certain cantons it is done in every detail. Doing this, the Swiss are moving rapidly in practically grappling with social problems that elsewhere are hardly more than speculative topics with scholars and theorists. In other countries, consequently, interested lookers-on, having from different points of view taken notes of democratic Switzerland, are, through newspaper, magazine, and book, describing its unprecedented progress and suggesting to their own countrymen what in Swiss governmental experience may be found of value at home. Of the more solid writing of this character, four books may especially be recommended. I mention them in the order of their publication.

"The Swiss Confederation." By Sir Francis Ottiwell Adams and C. D. Cunningham. (London: Macmillan & Co.; 1889; 289 pages; $1.75.) Sir Francis Ottiwell Adams was for some years British Minister at Berne.

"The Federal Government of Switzerland: An Essay on the Constitution." By Bernard Moses, Ph. D., professor of history and political economy, University of California. (Pacific Press Publishing Company: Oakland, Cal.; 1889; 256 pages; $1.25.) This work is largely a comparative study of constitutions. It is meant chiefly for the use of students of law and of legal history. It abounds, however, in facts as to Switzerland which up to the time of its publication were quite inaccessible to American readers.

"State and Federal Government of Switzerland." By John Martin Vincent, Ph. D., librarian and instructor in the department of history and politics, Johns Hopkins University. (Baltimore: Johns Hopkins Press; 1891; 247 pages; $1.50.) Professor Vincent had access, at the university, to the considerable collection of books and papers relating to Switzerland made by Professor J. C. Bluntschli, an eminent Swiss historian who died in 1881, and also to a large number of government publications presented by the Swiss Federal Council to the university library.

" The Swiss Republic." By Boyd Winchester, late United States Minister at Berne. (Philadelphia : J. B. Lippincott & Co.; 1891 ; 487 pages ; $1.50.) Mr. Winchester was stationed four years at Berne, and hence had better opportunity than Professor Vincent or Professor Moses for obtaining a thorough acquaintance with Switzerland. Much of his book is taken up with descriptive writing, all good.

Were I asked which of these four works affords the fullest information as to new Switzerland and new Swiss political methods, I should be obliged to refer the inquirer to his own needs. Professor Moses's is best for one applying himself to law and constitutional history. Professor Vincent's is richest in systematized details and statistics, especially such as relate to the Referendum and taxation ; and in it also is a bibliography of Swiss politics and history. For the general reader, desiring description of the country, stirring democratic sentiment, and an all-round view of the great little republic, Mr. Winchester's is preferable.

In expanding and rearranging my " Times " and " Chautauquan " articles, I have, to some extent, used these books.

Throughout this work, wherever possible, conservatives, rather than myself, have been made to speak ; hence quotations are frequent. The first draft of the chapters on Switzerland have been read by Swiss radicals of different schools, and the final proofsheets have been revised by a Swiss writer of repute living in New York ; therefore serious error is hardly probable. The one fault I myself have to find with the work is its baldness of statement, rendered necessary by space limits. I could, perhaps more easily, have prepared four or five hundred pages instead of the one hundred and twenty. I leave it rather to the reader to supply comparison and analysis and the eloquent comment of which, it seems to me, many of the statements of fact are worthy.   J. W. S.

THE INITIATIVE AND REFERENDUM IN SWITZERLAND.

Democratic versus Representative Government.

There is a radical difference between a democracy and a representative government. In a democracy, the citizens themselves make the law and superintend its administration ; in a representative government, the citizens empower legislators and executive officers to make the law and to carry it out. Under a democracy, sovereignty remains uninterruptedly with the citizens, or rather a changing majority of the citizens ; under a representative government, sovereignty is surrendered by the citizens, for stated terms, to officials. In other words, democracy is direct rule by the majority, while representative government is rule by a succession of quasi-oligarchies, indirectly and remotely responsible to the majority.

Observe, now, first, the influences that chiefly contribute to make government in the United States what it is :—

The county, state, and federal governments are not democracies. In form, they are quasi-oligarchies composed of representatives and executives ; but in fact they are frequently complete oligarchies, composed in part of unending rings of politicians that directly control the law and the offices, and in part of the permanent plutocracy, who purchase legislation through the politicians.

Observe, next, certain strong influences for the better that obtain in a pure democracy :—

An obvious influence is, in one respect, the same as that which enriches the plutocrat and prompts the politician to reach for power—self-interest. When all the members of any body of men find themselves in equal relation to a profitable end in which they solely are concerned, they will surely be inclined to assert their joint independence of other bodies in that respect, and, further, each member will claim his full share of whatever benefits arise. • But, more than that ; something like equality of benefits being achieved, perhaps through various agencies of force, a second influence will be brought powerfully to bear on those concerned. It is that of justice. Fair play to all the members will be generally demanded.

In a pure democracy, therefore, intelligently controlled self-interest and a consequent sentiment of justice are the sources in which the highest possible social benefits may be expected to begin.

The reader has now before him the political principle to be here maintained—pure democracy as distinguished from representative government. My argument, then, becomes this : To show that, by means of the one lawmaking method to which pure democracy is restricted,—that of direct legislation by the citizenship,—the political "ring," "boss," and "heeler" may be abolished, the American plutocracy destroyed, and government simplified and reduced to the limits set by the conscience of the majority as affected by social necessities. My task involves proof that direct legislation is possible with large communities.

Direct Legislation in Switzerland.

Evidence as to the practicability and the effects of direct legislation is afforded by Switzerland, especially in its history during the past twenty-five years. To this evidence I turn at once.

There are in Switzerland twenty-two cantons (states), which are subdivided into 2,706 communes (townships). The commune is the political as well as territorial unit. Commonly, as nearly as consistent with cantonal and federal rights, in local affairs the commune governs itself. Its citizens regard it as their smaller state. It is jealous of interference by the greater state. It has its own property to look after. Until the interests of the canton or the Confederation manifestly replace those of the immediate locality, the commune declines to part with the administration of its lands, forests, police, roads, schools, churches, or taxes.

In German Switzerland the adult male inhabitants of the commune meet at least once annually, usually in the town market place or on a mountain plain, and carry out their functions as citizens. There they debate proposed laws, name officers, and discuss affairs of a public nature. On such occasions, every citizen is a legislator, his voice and vote influencing the questions at issue. The right of initiating a measure belongs to each.   Decision is ordinarily made by show of hands.   In most cantons the youth becomes a voter at twenty, the legal age for acquiring a vote in federal affairs, though the range for cantonal matters is from eighteen to twenty-one.

Similar democratic legislative meetings govern two cantons as cantons and two other cantons divided into demi-cantons.   In the demi-canton of Outer Appenzell, 13,500 voters are qualified thus to meet and legislate, and the number actually assembled is sometimes 10,000.   But this is the highest extreme for such an assemblage—a Landsgemeinde (a land-community)— the lowest for a canton or a demi-canton comprising about 3,000.   One other canton (Schwyz, 50,307 inhabitants) has Landsgemeinde meetings, there being six, with an average of 2,000 voters to each.   In communal political assemblages, however, there are usually but a few hundred voters.

The yearly cantonal or demi-cantonal Landsgemeinde takes place on a Sunday in April or May. While the powers and duties of the body vary somewhat in different cantons, they usually cover the following subjects: Partial as well as total revision of the constitution ; enactment of all laws ; imposition of direct taxes ; incurrence of state debts and alienation of public domains ; the granting of public privileges ; assumption of foreigners into state citizenship ; establishment of new offices and the regulation of salaries : election of state, executive, and judicial officers.*

---

* J. M. Vincent : "State and Federal Government in Switzerland."

The programme for the meeting is arranged by the officials and published beforehand, the law in some cantons requiring publication four weeks before the meeting, and in others but ten days. "To give opportunities for individuals and authorities to make proposals and offer bills, the official gazette announces every January that for fourteen days after a given date petitions may be presented for that purpose. These must be written, the object plainly stated and accompanied by the reasons. All such motions are considered by what is called the Triple Council, or legislature, and are classified as 'expedient' and 'inexpedient.' A proposal receiving more than ten votes must be placed on the list of expedient, accompanied by the opinion of the council. The rejected are placed under a special rubric, familiarly called by the people the *Beiwagen*. The assembly may reverse the action of the council if it chooses and take a measure out of the 'extra coach,' but consideration of it is in that case deferred until the next year. In the larger assemblies debate is excluded, the vote being simply on rejection or adoption. In the smaller states the line is not so tightly drawn. . . . Votes are taken by show of hands, though secret ballot may be had if demanded, elections of officers following the same rule in this matter as legislation. Nominations for office, however, need not be sent in by petition, but may be offered by any one on the spot."*

---

* Vincent.

The Initiative and the Referendum.

It will be observed that the basic practical principles of both the communal meeting and the Landsgemeinde are these two :

(1) That every citizen shall have the right to propose a measure of law to his fellow-citizens—this principle being known as the Initiative.

(2) That the majority shall actually enact the law by voting the acceptance or the rejection of the measures proposed. This principle, when applied in non-Landsgemeinde cantons, through ballotings at polling places, on measures sent from legislative bodies to the people, is known as the Referendum.

The Initiative has been practiced in many of the communes and in the several Landsgemeinde cantons in one form or other from time immemorial. In the past score of years, however, it has been practiced by petition in an increasing number of the cantons not having the democratic assemblage of all the citizens.

The Referendum owes its origin to two sources. One source was in the vote taken at the communal meeting and the Landsgemeinde. The principle sometimes extended to cities, Berne, for instance, in the fifty-five years from 1469 to 1524, taking sixty referendary votings. The other source was in the vote taken by the ancient cantons on any action by their delegates to the federal Diet, or congress, these delegates undertaking no affair except on condition of referring it to the cantonal councils—*ad referendum.*

The principles of the Initiative and Referendum have of recent years been extended so as to apply, to a greater or lesser extent, not only to cantonal affairs in cantons far too large for the Landsgemeinde, but to certain affairs of the Swiss Confederation, comprising three million inhabitants. In other words, the Swiss nation today sees clearly, first, that the democratic system has manifold advantages over the representative ; and, secondly, that no higher degree of political freedom and justice can be obtained than by granting to the least practicable minority the legal right to propose a law and to the majority the right to accept or reject it. In enlarging the field of these working principles, the Swiss have developed in the political world a factor which, so far as it is in operation, is creating a revolution to be compared only with that caused in the industrial world by the steam engine.

The cantonal Initiative exists in fourteen of the twenty-two cantons—in some of them, however, only in reference to constitutional amendments. Usually, the proposal of a measure of cantonal law by popular initiative must be made through petition by from one-twelfth to one-sixteenth of the voters of the canton. When the petition reaches the cantonal legislature, the latter body is obliged, within a brief period, specified by the constitution, to refer the proposal to a cantonal vote. If the decision of the citizens is then favorable, the measure is law, and the executive and judicial officials must proceed to carry it into effect.

The cantonal Referendum is in constant practice in all the cantons except Freiburg, which is governed by a representative legislature. The extent, however, to which the Referendum is applied varies considerably. In two cantons it is applicable only to financial measures; in others it is optional with the people, who sometimes demand it, but oftener do not; in others it is obligatory in connection with the passage of every law. More explicitly: In the canton of Vaud a mere pseudo-referendary right exists, under which the Grand Council (the legislature) may, if it so decides, propose a reference to the citizens. Valais takes a popular vote only on such propositions passed by the Grand Council as involve a one and a half per cent increase in taxation or a total expenditure of 60,000 francs. With increasing confidence in the people, the cantons of Lucerne, Zug, Bâle City, Schaffhausen, St. Gall, Ticino, Neuchâtel, and Geneva refer a proposed law, after it has passed the Grand Council, to the voters when a certain proportion of the citizens, usually one-sixth to one-fourth, demand it by formal petition. This form is called the optional Referendum. Employed to its utmost in Zurich, Schwyz, Berne, Soleure, Bâle Land, Aargau, Thurgau, and the Grisons, in these cantons the Referendum permits no law to be passed or expenditure beyond a stipulated sum to be made by the legislature without a vote of the people. This is known as the obligatory Referendum. Glarus, Uri, the half cantons of Niwald and Obwald (Unterwald), and those of Outer and Inner

Appenzell, as cantons, or demi-cantons, still practice the democratic assemblage—the Landsgemeinde.

In the following statistics, the reader may see at a glance the progress of the Referendum to the present date, with the population of Switzerland by cantons, and the difficulties presented by differences of language in the introduction of reforms :—

Canton.	No. inhab. Dec., 1888.	Language.	Form of Passing Laws.	Yr. of Entry
Zurich . . .	337,183	German.	Oblig. Ref.	1351
Berne . . .	536,679	Ger. and French.	"	1353
Lucerne. . .	135,360	German.	Optional Ref.	1332
Uri	17,249	Ger. and Italian.	Landsgemeinde.	1291
Schwyz . .	50,307	German.	Oblig. Ref.	"
Unterwald				"
Obwald . .	15,041	"	Landsgemeinde.	
Niwald . .	12,538	"	"	
Glarus . . .	33,825	"	"	1352
Zug	23,029	"	Optional Ref.	"
Freiburg . .	119,155	French and Ger.	Legislature.	1481
Soleure . . .	85,621	German.	Oblig. Ref.	"
Bâle				1501
City . . .	73,749	"	Optional Ref.	
Country . .	61,941	"	Oblig. Ref.	
Schaffhausen	37,783	"	Optional Ref.	"
Appenzell				1573
Outer . .	54,109	"	Landsgemeinde.	
Inner . .	12,888	"	"	
St. Gall . .	228,160	"	Optional Ref.	1803
Grisons . .	94,810	Ger., Ital., Rom.	Oblig. Ref.	"
Aargau . .	193,580	German.	"	"
Thurgau . .	104,678	"	"	"
Ticino . . .	126,751	Italian.	Optional Ref.	"
Vaud. . . .	247,655	French and Ger.	"	"
Valais . . .	101,985	"	Finance Ref.	1814
Neuchâtel . .	108,153	French.	Optional Ref.	"
Geneva . . .	105,509	"	"	"
	2,917,740			

In round numbers, 2,092,000 of the Swiss people speak German, 637,000 French, 156,000 Italian, and 30,000 Romansch. Of the principal cities, in 1887, Zurich, with suburbs, had 92,685 inhabitants ; Bâle, 73,-963 ; Geneva, with suburbs, 73,504 ; Berne, 50,220 ; Lausanne, 32,954 ; and five others from 17,000 to 25,000. Fourteen per cent of the inhabitants (410,000) live in cities of more than 15,000. The factory workers number 161,000, representing about half a million inhabitants, and the peasant proprietors nearly 260,000, representing almost two millions. The area of Switzerland is 15,892 square miles,—slightly in excess of double that of New Jersey. The population is slightly less than that of Ohio.

Switzerland—The Youngest of Republics.

It is misleading to suppose, as is often done, that the Switzerland of today is the republic which has stood for six hundred years. In truth, it is the youngest of republics. Its chief governmental features, cantonal and federal, are the work of the present generation. Its unique executive council, its democratic army organization, its republican railway management, its federal post-office, its system of taxation, its two-chambered congress, the very Confederation itself —all were originated in the constitution of 1848, the first that was anything more than a federal compact. The federal Referendum began only in 1874. The federal Initiative has been just adopted (1891.)*The form of cantonal Referendum now practiced was but begun (in St. Gall) in 1830, and forty years ago only five cantons had any Referendum whatever, and these in the optional form. It is of very recent years that

* For   constitutional amendments only.

the movement has become steady toward the general adoption of the cantonal Referendum. In 1860 but 34 per cent of the Swiss possessed it, 66 per cent delegating their sovereign rights to representatives. But in 1870 the referendariship had risen to 71 per cent, only 29 submitting to lawmaking officials ; and today the proportions are more than 90 per cent to less than 10.

The thoughtful reader will ask : Why this continual progress toward a purer democracy ? Wherein lie the inducements to this persistent revolution ?

The answer is this : The masses of the citizens of Switzerland found it necessary to revolt against their plutocracy and the corrupt politicians who were exploiting the country through the representative system. For a peaceful revolution these masses found the means in the working principles of their communal meetings—the Initiative and Referendum,—and these principles they are applying throughout the republic as fast as circumstances admit.*

The great movement for democracy in Europe that culminated in the uprising of 1848 brought to the front many original men, who discussed innovations in government from every radical point of view. Among these thinkers were Martin Rittinghausen, Emile Girardin, and Louis Blanc. From September, 1850, to December, 1851, the date of the *coup d'état* of Louis Bonaparte, these reformers discussed, in the " Democratie

---

* While the reports of the Secretary of State and "The History of the Referendum," by Th. Curti, will bear out many of the statements here made as to how the change from representative to direct legislation came about, the story as I give it has been written me by Herr Carl Bürkli, of Zurich, known in his canton as the " Father of the Referendum."

pacifique," a weekly newspaper of Paris, the subject of direct legislation by the citizens. Their essays created a sensation in France, and more than thirty journals actively supported the proposed institution, when the *coup d'état* put an end to free speech. The articles were reprinted in book form in Brussels, and other works on the subject were afterward issued by Rittinghausen and his co-worker Victor Considérant. Among Considérant's works was "Solution, ou gouvernement direct du peuple," and this and companion works that fell into the hands of Carl Bürkli convinced the latter and other citizens of Zurich ("an unknown set of men," says Bürkli) of the practicability of the democratic methods advocated. The subject was widely agitated and studied in Switzerland, and the fact that the theory was already to some extent in practice there (and in ancient times had been much practiced) led to further experiments, and these, attaining success, to further, and thus the work has gone on. The cantonal Initiative was almost unknown outside the Landsgemeinde when it was established in Zurich in 1869. Soon, however, through it and the obligatory Referenendum (to use Herr Bürkli's words) : " The plutocratic government and the Grand Council of Zurich, which had connived with the private banks and railroads, were pulled down in one great voting swoop. The people had grown tired of being beheaded by the office-holders after every election." And politicians and the privileged classes have ever since been going down before these instruments in the hands of the people. The doctrines of the French theorists needed but to be engrafted on ancient Swiss custom, the Frenchmen in fact having drawn upon Swiss experience.

The Optional and the Obligatory Referendum.

To-day the movement in the Swiss cantons is not only toward the Referendum, but toward its obligatory form. The practice of the optional form has revealed defects in it which are inherent.*

Geneva's management of the optional cantonal Referendum is typical. The constitution provides that, certain of the laws being excepted from the Referendum, and a prerequisite of its operation being the presentation to the Grand Council of a popular petition, the people may sanction or reject not only the bulk of the laws passed by the Grand Council but also the decrees issued by the legislative and executive powers. The exceptions are (1) "measures of urgence" and (2) the items of the annual budget, save such as establish a new tax, increase one in force, or necessitate an issue of bonds. The Referendum cannot be exercised against the budget as a whole, the Grand Council indicating the sections which are to go to public vote. In case of opposition to any measure, a petition for the Referendum is put in circulation. To prevent the measure from becoming law, the petition must receive the legally attested signatures of at least 3,500 citizens —about one in six of the cantonal vote—within thirty

---

* The facts relative to the operation of these two forms of the Referendum have been given me by Monsieur P. Jamin, of Geneva.

days after the publication of the proposed measure. After this period—known as "the first delay"—the referendary vote, if the petition has been successful, must take place within forty days—"the second delay."

The power of declaring measures to be "of urgence" lies with the Grand Council, the body passing the measures. Small wonder, then, that in its eyes many bills are of too much and too immediate importance to go to the people. "The habit," protested Grand Councilor M. Putet, on one occasion, "tends more and more to introduce itself here of decreeing urgence unnecessarily, thus taking away from the Referendum expenses which have nothing of urgence. This is contrary to the spirit of the constitutional law. Public necessity alone can authorize the Grand Council to take away any of its acts from the public control."

Another defect in the optional Referendum is that it can be transformed into a partisan weapon—politicians being ready, in Geneva, as in San Francisco, to take advantage of the law for party purposes. For example, the representatives of a minority party, seeking a concession from a majority which has just passed a bill, will threaten, if their demands are not granted, to agitate for the Referendum on the bill; this, though the minority itself may favor the measure, some of its members, perhaps, having voted for it. As the majority may be uncertain of the outcome of a struggle at the polls, it will probably be inclined to make peace on the terms dictated by the minority.

But the most serious objections to the optional form arise in connection with the petitioning. Easy though it be for a rich and strong party to bear the expense of printing, mailing, and distributing petitions and circulars, in case of opposition from the poorer classes the cost may prove an insurmountable obstacle. Especially is it difficult to get up a petition after several successive appeals coming close together, the constant agitation growing tiresome as well as financially burdensome. Hence, measures have sometimes become law simply because the people have not had time to recover from the prolonged agitation in connection with preceding propositions. Besides, each measure submitted to the optional Referendum brings with it two separate waves of popular discussion—one on the petition and one on the subsequent vote. On this point ex-President Numa Droz has said: "The agitation which takes place while collecting the necessary signatures, nearly always attended with strong feeling, diverts the mind from the object of the law, perverts in advance public opinion, and, not permitting later the calm discussion of the measure proposed, establishes an almost irresistible current toward rejection." Finally, a fact as notorious in Switzerland as vote-buying in America, a large number of citizens who are hostile to a proposed law may fear to record an adverse opinion by signing a Referendum list. Their signatures may be seen and the unveiling of their sentiments imperil their means of livelihood.

Zurich furnishes the example of the cantons having

the obligatory Referendum. There the law provides:
1. That all laws, decrees, and changes in the constitution must be submitted to the people. 2. That
all decisions of the Grand Council on existing law
must be voted on. 3. That the Grand Council may
submit decisions which it itself proposes to make,
and that, besides the voting on the whole law, the
Council may ask a vote on a special point. The Grand
Council cannot put in force provisionally any law or
decree. The propositions must be sent to the voters
at least thirty days before voting. The regular referendary ballotings take place twice a year, spring and
autumn, but in urgent cases the Grand Council may
call for a special election. The law in this canton
assists the lawmakers—the voters—in their task;
when a citizen is casting his own vote he may also
deposit that of one or two relatives and friends, upon
presenting their electoral card or a certificate of au-
thorization.

In effect, the obligatory Referendum makes of the
entire citizenship a deliberative body in perpetual session—this end being accomplished in Zurich in the
face of every form of opposing argument. Formerly,
its adversaries made much of the fact that it was ever
calling the voters to the urns ; but this is now avoided
by the semi-annual elections. It was once feared that
party tickets would be voted without regard to the
merits of the various measures submitted ; but it has
been proved beyond doubt that the fate of one proposition has no effect whatever on that of another decid-

ed at the same time. Zurich has pronounced on nine-
ty-one laws in twenty-eight elections, the votes indicating surprising independence of judgment. When
the obligatory form was proposed for Zurich, its sup-
porters declared it a sure instrument, but that it might
prove a costly one they were not prepared by experiment to deny. Now, however, they have the data to
show that taxes—unfailing reflexes of public expenditure—are lower than ever, those for police, for example,
being only about half those of optional Geneva, a less
populous canton. To the prophets who foresaw endless partisan strife in case the Referendum was to be
called in force on every measure, Zurich has replied by
reducing partisanship to its feeblest point, the people
indifferent to parties since an honest vote of the
whole body of citizens must be the final issue of
every question.

The people of Zurich have proved that the science
of politics is simple. By refusing special legislation,
they evade a flood of bills. By deeming appropriations once revised as in most part necessary, they pay
attention chiefly to new items. By establishing principles in law, they forbid violations. Thus there remain no profound problems of state, no abstruse questions as to authorities, no conflict as to what is the
law. Word fresh from the people is law.

The Federal Referendum.

The Federal Referendum, first established by the
constitution of 1874, is optional. The demand for it

must be made by 30,000 citizens or by eight cantons. The petition for a vote under it must be made within ninety days after the publication of the proposed law. It is operative with respect either to a statute as passed by the Federal Assembly (congress), or a decree of the executive power. Of 149 Federal laws and decrees subject to the Referendum passed up to the close of 1891 under the constitution of 1874, twenty-seven were challenged by the necessary 30,000 petitioners, fifteen being rejected and twelve accepted. The Federal Initiative was established by a vote taken on Sunday, July 5, 1891. It requires 50,000 petitioners, whose proposal must be discussed by the Federal assembly and then sent within a prescribed delay to the whole citizenship for a vote. The Initiative is not a petition to the legislative body; it is a demand made on the entire citizenship.

Where the cantonal Referendum is optional, a successful petition for it frequently secures a rejection of the law called in question.   In 1862 and again in 1878, the canton of Geneva rejected proposed changes in its constitution, on the latter occasion by a majority of 6,000 in a vote of 11,000. Twice since 1847 the same canton has decided against an increase of official salaries, and lately it has declined to reduce the number of its executive councilors from seven to five. The experience of the Confederation has been similar. Between 1874 and 1880 five measures recommended by the Federal Executive and passed by the Federal Assembly were vetoed by a national vote.

Revision of Constitutions.

Revision of a constitution through the popular vote is common. Since 1814, there have been sixty revisions by the people of cantonal constitutions alone. Geneva asks its citizens every fifteen years if they wish to revise their organic law, thus twice in a generation practically determining whether they are in this respect content. The Federal constitution · may be revised at any time. Fifty thousand voters petitioning for it, or the Federal Assembly (congress) demanding it, the question is submitted to the country. If the vote is in the affirmative, the Council of States (the senate) and the National Council (the house) are both dissolved. An election of these bodies takes place at once; the Assembly, fresh from the people, then makes the required revision and submits the revised constitution to the country. To stand, it must be supported by a majority of the voters and a majority of the twenty-two cantons.

Summary.

To sum up : In Switzerland, in this generation, direct legislation has in many respects been established for the federal government, while in so large a canton as Zurich, with nearly 340,000 inhabitants, it has also been made applicable to every proposed cantonal law, decree, and order,—the citizens of that canton themselves disposing by vote of all questions of taxation, public finance, executive acts, state employment, corporation grants, public works, and similar operations of government commonly, even in republican states, left to legislators and other officials. In every canton having the Initiative and the obligatory Referendum, all power has been stripped from the officials except that of a stewardship which is continually and minutely supervised and controlled by the voters. Moreover, it is possible that yet a few years and the affairs not only of every canton of Switzerland but of the Confederation itself will thus be taken in hand at every step.

Here, then, is evidence incontrovertible that pure democracy, through direct legislation by the citizenship, is practicable—more, is now practiced—in large communities. Next as to its effects, proven and probable.

THE PUBLIC STEWARDSHIP OF SWITZER-
LAND.

If it be conceived that the fundamental principles of a free society are these: That the bond uniting the citizens should be that of contract; that rights, including those in natural resources, should be equal, and that each producer should retain the full product of his toil, it must be conceded on examination that toward this ideal Switzerland has made further advances than any other country, despite notable points in exception and the imperfect form of its federal Initiative and Referendum. Before particulars are entered into, some general observations on this head may be made.

The Political Status in Switzerland.

An impressive fact in Swiss politics to-day is its peace. Especially is this true of the contents and tone of the press. In Italy and Austria, on the south and east, the newspapers are comparatively few, mostly feeble, and in general subservient to party or government; in Germany, on the north, where State Socialism is strong, the radical press is at times turbulent and the government journals reflect the despotism they uphold; in France, on the west and southwest, the public writers are ever busy over the successive unstable cen-

tral administrations at Paris, which exercise a bureau-
cratic direction of every commune in the land. In all
these countries, men rather than measures are the
objects of discussion, an immediate important campaign question inevitably being whether, when once in
office, candidates may make good their ante-election
promises. Thus, on all sides, over the border from
Switzerland, political turmoil, with its rancor, person-
alities, false reports, hatreds, and corruptions, is endless. But in Switzerland, debate uniformly bears not
on men but on measures. The reasons are plain.
Where the veto is possessed by the people, in vain may
rogues go to the legislature. With few or no party
spoils, attention to public business, and not to patron-
age or private privilege, is profitable to office holders
as well as to the political press.

In the number of newspapers proportionate to population, Switzerland stands with the United States
at the head of the statistical list for the world. In
their general character, Swiss political journals are
higher than American. They are little tempted to
knife reputations, to start false campaign issues, to
inflame partisan feeling; for every prospective cantonal measure undergoes sober popular discussion the
year round, with the certain vote of the citizenship in
view in the cantons having the Landsgemeinde or the
obligatory Referendum, and a possible vote in most of
the other cantons, while federal measures also may be
met with the federal optional Referendum.

The purity and peacefulness of Swiss press and

politics are due to the national development of today as expressed in appropriate institutions. Of these institutions the most effective, the fundamental, is direct legislation, accompanied as it is with general education. In education the Swiss are preëminent among nations. Illiteracy is at a lower percentage than in any other country ; primary instruction is free and compulsory in all the cantons ; and that the higher education is general is shown in the four universities, employing three hundred instructors.

An enlightened people, employing the ballot freely, directly, and in consequence effectively—this is the true sovereign governing power in Switzerland. As to what, in general terms, have been the effects of this power on the public welfare, as to how the Swiss themselves feel toward their government, and as to what are the opinions of foreign observers on the recent changes through the Initiative and Referendum, some testimony may at this point be offered.

In the present year, Mr. W. D. McCrackan has published in the "Arena" of Boston his observations of Swiss politics. He found, he says, the effects of the Referendum to be admirable. Jobbery and extravagance are unknown, and politics, as there is no money in it, has ceased to be a trade. The men elected to office are taken from the ranks of the citizens, and are chosen because of their fitness for the work. The people take an intelligent interest in every kind of local and federal legislation, and have a full sense of their political responsibility. The mass of useless or evil

laws which legislatures in other countries are constantly passing with little consideration, and which
have constantly to be repealed, are in Switzerland not
passed at all.

In a study of the direct legislation of Switzerland,
the "Westminster Review," February, 1888, passed this
opinion : "The bulk of the people move more slowly
than their representatives, are more cautious in adopting new and trying legislative experiments, and have
a tendency to reject propositions submitted to them
for the first time." Further: "The issue which is presented to the sovereign people is invariably and neces-
sarily reduced to its simplest expression, and so placed
before them as to be capable of an affirmative or nega-
tive answer. In practice, therefore, the discussion of details is left to the representative assemblies, while the
people express approval or disapproval of the general
principle or policy embraced in the proposed measure.
Public attention being confined to the issue, leaders
are nothing. The collective wisdom judges of merits."

A. V. Dicey, the critic of constitutions, writes in the
"Nation," October 8, 1885 : "The Referendum must be
considered, on the whole, a conservative arrangement.
It tends at once to hinder rapid change and also to get
rid of that inflexibility or immutability which, in the
eyes of Englishmen at least, is a defect in the constitution of the United States."

A Swiss radical has written me as follows : "The
development given to education during the last quar-

ter of a century will have without doubt as a consequence an improved judgment on the part of a large
number of electors. The press also has a rôle more
preponderant than formerly. Everybody reads. Certainly the ruling classes profit largely by the power of
the printing press, but with the electors who have received some instruction the capitalist newspapers are
taken with due allowance for their sincerity. Their
opinion is not accepted without inquiry. We see a
rapid development of ideas, if not completely new, at
least renewed and more widespread. More or less
radical reviews and periodicals, in large number, are
not without influence, and their appearance proves
that great changes are imminent."

Professor Dicey has contrasted the Referendum with
the *plébiscite* : " The Referendum looks at first sight like
a French *plébiscite*, but no two institutions can be
marked by more essential differences. The *plébiscite* is
a revolutionary or at least abnormal proceeding. It is
not preceded by debate. The form and nature of the
questions to be submitted to the nation are chosen and
settled by the men in power, and Frenchmen are asked
whether they will or will not accept a given policy.
Rarely, indeed, when it has been taken, has the voting
itself been full or fair. Deliberation and discussion
are the requisite conditions for rational decision.
Where effective opposition is an impossibility, nominal assent is an unmeaning compliment. These essential characteristics, the lack of which deprives
a French *plébiscite* of all moral significance, are the

undoubted properties of the Swiss Referendum.'

In the "Revue des Deux Mondes," Paris, August, 1801, Louis Wuarin, an interested observer of Swiss politics for many years, writes: "A people may indicate its will, not from a distance, but near at hand, always superintending the work of its agents, watching them, stopping them if there is reason for so doing, constraining them, in a word, to carry out the people's will in both legislative and administrative affairs. In this form of government the representative system is reduced to a minimum. The deliberative bodies resemble simple committees charged with preparing work for an elected assembly, and here the elected assembly is replaced by the people. This sovereign action in person in the transaction of public business may extend more or less widely; it may be limited to the State, or it may be extended to the province also, and even to the town. To whatever extent this supervision of the people may go, one thing may certainly be expected, which is that the supervision will become closer and closer as time goes on. It never has been known that citizens gave up willingly and deliberately rights acquired, and the natural tendency of citizens is to increase their privileges. Switzerland is an example of this type of democratic government. . . . There is some reason for regarding parliamentary government—at least under its classic and orthodox form of rivalry between two parties, who watch each other closely, in order to profit by the faults of their adversaries, who dispute with each other for power without the interests of the country, in the ardor of the encounter, being always considered—as a transitory form in the evolution of democracy."

The spirit of the Swiss law and its relation to the liberty of the individual are shown in passages of the cantonal and federal constitutions. That of Uri declares: "Whatever the Landsgemeinde, within the limits of its competence, ordains, is law of the land, and as such shall be obeyed," but : "The guiding principle of the Landsgemeinde shall be justice and the welfare of the fatherland, not willfulness nor the power of the strongest." That of Zurich : "The people exercise the lawmaking power, with the assistance of the state legislature." That of the Confederation : "All the Swiss people are equal before the law. There are in Switzerland no subjects, nor privileges of place, birth, persons, or families."

In these general notes and quotations is sketched in broad lines the political environment of the Swiss citizen of to-day. The social mind with which he stands in contact is politically developed, is bent on justice, is accustomed to look for safe results from the people's laws, is at present more than ever inclined to trust direct legislation, and, on the whole, is in a state of calmness, soberness, tolerance, and political self-discipline.

The machinery of public stewardship, subject to popular guidance, may now be traced, beginning with the most simple form.

Organization of the Commune.

The common necessities of a Swiss neighborhood, such as establishing and maintaining local roads, police, and schools, and administering its common wealth, bring its citizens together in democratic assemblages. These are of different forms.

One form of such assemblage, the basis of the superstructure of government, is the political communal meeting. " In it take place the elections, federal, state, and local ; it is the local unit of state government and the residuary legatee of all powers not granted to other authorities. Its procedure is ample and highly democratic. It meets either at the call of an executive council of its own election, or in pursuance of adjournment, and, as a rule, on a Sunday or holiday. Its presiding officer is sometimes the *maire*, sometimes a special chairman. Care is taken that only voters shall sit in the body of the assembly, it being a rule in Zurich that the register of citizens shall lie on the desk for inspection. Tellers are appointed by vote and must be persons who do not belong to the village council, since that is the local cabinet which proposes measures for consideration. Any member of the assembly may offer motions or amendments, but usually they are brought forward by the town council, or at least referred to that body before being voted upon."* The officials of the commune chosen in the communal meeting, are one chief executive (who in French communes usually has two assistants), a communal coun-

* Vincent.

cil, which legislates on the lesser matters coming up between communal meetings, and such minor officials as are not left to the choice of the council.

A second form of neighborhood assemblage is one composed only of those citizens who have rights in the communal corporate domains and funds, these rights being either inherited or acquired (sometimes by purchase) after a term of purely political citizenship.

A third form is the parish meeting, at which gather the members of the same faith in the commune, or of even a smaller church district. The Protestant, the Catholic, and the Jewish are recognized as State religions—the Protestant alone in some cantons, the Catholic in others, both in several, and both with the Jewish in others.

A fourth form of local assembly is that of the school district, usually a subdivision of a commune. It elects a board of education, votes taxes to defray school expenses, supervises educational matters, and in some districts elects teachers.

Dividing the commune thus into voting groups, each with its appropriate purpose, makes for justice. He who has a share in the communal public wealth (forests, pastoral and agricultural lands, and perhaps funds), is not endangered in this property through the votes of non-participant newcomers. Nor are educational affairs mixed with general politics. And, though State and religion are not yet severed, each form of belief is largely left to itself; in some cantons provision is

made that a citizen's taxes shall not go toward the
support of a religion to which he is opposed.

Organization of Canton and Confederation.

In no canton in Switzerland is there more than one
legislative body : in none is there a senate. The cities
of Switzerland have no mayor, the cantons have no
governor, and, if the title be used in the American
sense, the republic has no President. Instead of the
usual single executive head, the Swiss employ an executive council. Hence, 'n every canton a deadlock
in legislation is impossible, the way is open for all
law demanded by a majority, and neither in canton
nor Confederation is one-man power known.

The cantonal legislature is the Grand Council. In
the Landsgemeinde cantons and those having the
obligatory Referendum, it is little more than a super-
visory committee, preparing measures for the vote of
the citizens and acting as a check on the cantonal executive council. In the remaining cantons (those having the optional Referendum), the legislature has
the power to spend money below a specified limit ; to
enact laws of specified kinds, usually not of general
application ; and to elect the more important officials,
the amount of discretion [in the different cantons] ris-
ing gradually till the complete representative government is reached "* in Freiburg, which resembles one
of our states. Though in several cantons the Grand
Council meets every two months for a few days' ses-

* Vincent.

sion, in most of the cantons it meets twice a year. The pay of members ranges from sixty cents to $1.20 per day. The legislative bodies are large; the ratio in five cantons is one legislator to every 1,000 inhabitants; in twelve it ranges from one to 187 up to one to 800, and in the remaining five from one to 1,000 to one to 2,000. The Landsgemeinde cantons usually have fifty to sixty members; Geneva, with 20,000 voters, has a hundred.

In six of the twenty-two cantons, if a certain number of voters petition for it, the question must be submitted to the people whether or not the legislature shall be recalled and a new one elected.

The formation of the Swiss Federal Assembly (congress), established in 1848, was influenced by the make-up of the American congress. The lower house is elected by districts, as in the United States, the basis of representation being one member to 20,000 inhabitants, and the number of members 147. The term for this house is three years; the pay; four dollars a day, during session, and mileage. The upper house, the Council of States (senate), the only body of the kind in Switzerland, is composed of two members from each canton. Cantonal law governing their election, the tenure of their office is not the same : in some cantons they are elected by the people, in others by the legislature ; their pay varies ; their term of office ranges from one to three years. Their brief terms and the fact that their more important functions, such as the election of the federal executive council, take place in joint session with the second chamber, render the members of the "upper" house of less weight in national affairs than those of the "lower."

Swiss Executives.

The executive councils of the cities, the cantons, and the Confederation are all of one form.   They are committees, composed of members of equal rank.   The number of members varies.   Of cantonal executive councilors, there are seven in eleven of the cantons, three, five, and nine in others, and eleven in one.   In addition to carrying out the law, the executive council usually assists somewhat in legislation, the members not only introducing but speaking upon measures in the legislative body with which they are associated, without, however, having a vote.   In about half the cantons, the cantonal executive councils are elected by the people ; in the rest by the legislative body.

Types of the executive councils are those of Geneva, city and canton.   The city executive council is composed of five members, elected by the people for four years.   The salary of its president is $800 a year ; that of the other four members, $600.   The cantonal executive has seven members ; the salaries are : the president, $1,200 ; the rest, $1,000.   In both city and cantonal councils each member is the head of an administrative department.   The cantonal executive council has the power to suspend the deliberations of the city executive council and those of the communal councils whenever in its judgment these bodies transcend their legal powers or refuse to conform to the law.   In case

of such suspension, a meeting of the cantonal Grand
Council (the legislature) must be called within a week,
and if it approves of the action of the cantonal executive, the council suspended is dissolved, and an election for another must be had within a month, the
members of the body dissolved not being immediately
eligible for re-election. The cantonal executive council may also revoke the commissions of communal executives (maires and adjoints), who then cannot immediately be re-elected. Check to the extensive powers
of the cantonal executive council lies in the fact that
its members are elected directly by the people and
hold office for only two years. But in cantons having
the obligatory Referendum, Geneva's methods, however advanced in the eyes of American republicans,
are not regarded as strictly democratic.

The Federal Executive Council.

The Swiss nation has never placed one man at its
head. Prior to 1848, executive as well as legislative
powers were vested in the one house of the Diet. Under the constitution adopted in that year, with which
the Switzerland as now organized really began, the
present form of the executive was established.

This executive is the Federal Council, a board of
seven members, whose term is three years, and who
are elected in joint session by the two houses of the
Federal Assembly (congress). The presiding officer
of the council, chosen as such by the Federal Assembly, is elected for one year. He cannot be his own

successor. While he is nominally President of the
Confederation, Swiss treatises on the subject uniformly emphasize the fact that he is actually no more than
chairman of the executive council.   He is but "first
among his equals" (*primus inter pares*).   His prerogatives
—thus to describe whatever powers fall within his duties—are no greater than those pertaining to the rest
of the board.   Unlike the President of the United
States, he has no rank in the army, no power of veto,
no influence with the judiciary ; he cannot appoint
military commanders, or independently name any officials whatever ; he cannot enforce a policy, or declare
war, or make peace, or conclude a treaty.   His name
is not a by-word in his own country.   Not a few among
the intelligent Swiss would pause a moment to recall
his name if suddenly asked : " Who is President this
year ?"

  The federal executive council is elected on the as-
sembling of the Federal Assembly after the triennial
election for members of the lower house.   All Swiss
citizens are eligible, except that no two members may
be chosen from the same canton.   The President's salary is $2,605, that of the other members $2,316.   While
in office, the councilors may not perform any other
public function, engage in any kind of trade, or practice any profession.   A member of the council is at
the head of each department of the government, viz.:
Foreign Affairs, Interior, Justice and Police, Military,
Finances, Commerce and Agriculture, and Post-Office
and Railroads.   The constitution directs a joint trans-

action of the business of the council by all the seven members, with the injunction that responsibility and unity of action be not enfeebled. The council appoints employés and functionaries of the federal departments. Each member may present a nomination for any branch, but names are usually handed in by the head of the department in which the appointment is made. As a minority of the board is uniformly composed of members of the political party not, if it may be so described, "in power," purely partisan employments are difficult. Removals of federal office holders in order to repay party workers are unheard of.

The executive council may employ experts for special tasks, it has the right to introduce bills in the Federal Assembly, and each councilor has a "consultative voice" in both houses. In practice, the council is simply an executive commission expressing the will of the assembly, the latter having even ordered the revision of regulations drawn up by the council for its employés at Berne. The acts of the assembly being liable to the Referendum, connection with the will of the people is established. Thus popular sovereignty finally, and quite directly, controls.

While both legislators and executives are elected for short terms, it is customary for the same men to serve in public capacities a long time. Though the people may recall their servants at brief intervals, they almost invariably ask them to continue in service. Employés keep their places at their will during good behavior. This custom extends to the higher offices filled by appointment. One minister to Paris held the position for twenty-three years ; one to Rome, for sixteen. Once elected to the federal executive council, a public man may regard his office as a permanency. Of the council of 1889, one member had served since 1863, another since 1866. Up to 1879 no seat in the council had ever become vacant excepting through death or resignation.

Features of the Judiciary.

Civil and criminal courts are separate. The justice of the peace sits in a case first as arbitrator, and not until he fails in that capacity does he assume the chair of magistrate. His decision is final in cases involving sums up to a certain amount, varying in different localities. Two other grades of court are maintained in the canton, one sitting for a judicial subdivision called a district, and a higher court for the whole canton. Members of the district tribunal, consisting of five or seven members, are commonly elected by the people, their terms varying, with eight years as the longest. The judges of the cantonal courts as a rule are chosen by the Grand Council ; their number seven to thirteen ; their terms one to eight years. The cantonal court is the court of last resort. The Federal Tribunal, which consists of nine judges and nine alternates, elected for six years, tries cases between canton and canton or individual and canton. For this bench practically all Swiss citizens are eligible. The entire judicial system seems designed for the speedy trial of cases and the discouragement of litigation.

No court in Switzerland, not even the Federal Tribunal, can reverse the decisions of the Federal Assembly (congress). This can be done only by the people.

The election by the Assembly of the Federal Tribunal—as well as of the federal executive—has met with strong opposition. Before long both bodies may be elected by popular vote.

Swiss jurors are elected by the people and hold office six years. In French and German Switzerland, there is one such juror for every thousand inhabitants, and in Italian Switzerland one for every five hundred. To a Swiss it would seem as odd to select jurors haphazard as to so select judges.

In most of the manufacturing cantons, councils of prud'hommes are elected by the people. The various industries and professions are classified in ten groups, each of which chooses a council of prud'hommes composed of fifteen employers and fifteen employés. Each council is divided into a bureau of conciliation, a tribunal of prud'hommes, and a chamber of appeals, cases going on appeal from one board to another in the order named. These councils have jurisdiction only in the trades, their sessions relating chiefly to payment for services and contracts of apprenticeship.

A Democratic Army.

In surveying the simple political machinery of Switzerland, the inquirer, remembering the fate of so many republics, may be led to ask as to the danger of its overthrow by the Swiss army. The reply is that, here, again, so far as may be seen, the nation has wisely planned safeguards. To show how, and as the Swiss army differs widely from all others in its organization, some particulars regarding it are here pertinent.

The more important features of the Swiss military system, established in 1874, are as follows : There is no Commander-in-chief in time of peace. There is no aristocracy of officers. Pensions are fixed by law. There is no substitute system. Every citizen not disabled is liable either to military duty or to duties essential in time of war, such as service in the postal department, the hospitals, or the prisons. Citizens entirely disabled and unfit for the ranks or semi-military service are taxed to a certain per centage of their property or income. No canton is allowed to maintain more than three hundred men under arms without federal authority.

Though there is no standing army, every man in the country between the ages of seventeen and fifty is enrolled and subject annually either to drill or inspection. On January 1, 1891, the active army, comprising all unexempt citizens between twenty and thirty-two years, contained 126,444 officers and men ; the first reserve, thirty-three to forty-four years, 80,795 ; the second reserve, all others, 268,715 ; total, 475,955. The Confederation can place in the field in less than a week more than 200,000 men, armed, uniformed, drilled, and every man in his place.

On attaining his twentieth year, every Swiss youth

is summoned before a board of physicians and military officers for physical and mental examination. Those adjudged unfit for service are exempted—temporarily if the infirmity may pass away, for life if it be permanent. The tax on exempted men is $1.20 plus thirty cents per year for $200 of their wealth or $20 of their income, until the age of thirty-two years, and half these sums until the age of forty-four. On being enrolled in his canton, the soldier is allowed to return home. He takes with him his arms and accoutrements, and thenceforth is responsible for them. He is ever ready for service at short call. Intrusting the soldiery with their outfit reduces the number of armories, thus cutting down public expenditures and preventing loss through capture in case of sudden invasion by an enemy.

In the Swiss army are eight divisions of the active force and eight of the reserve, adjoining cantons uniting to form a division. Each summer one division is called out for the grand manœuvres, all being brought out once in the course of eight years.

In case of war a General is named by the Federal Assembly. At the head of the army in time of peace is a staff, composed of three colonels, sixteen lieutenant colonels and majors, and thirty-five captains.

The cost of maintaining the army is small, on an average $3,500,000 a year. Officers and soldiers alike receive pay only while in service. If wounded or taken ill on duty, a man in the ranks may draw up to $240 a year pension while suffering disability. Lesser

sums may be drawn by the family of a soldier who
loses his life in the service.

At Thoune, near Berne, is the federal military academy. It is open to any Swiss youth who can support
himself while there. Not even the President of the
Confederation may in time of peace propose any man
for a commission who has not studied at the Thoune
academy. A place as commissioned officer is not
sought for as a fat office nor as a ready stepping-stone
to social position. As a rule only such youths study
at Thoune as are inclined to the profession of arms.
Promotion is according to both merit and seniority.
Officers up to the rank of major are commissioned by
the cantons, the higher grades by the Confederation.

In Switzerland, then, the military leader appears
only when needed, in war ; he cannot for years afterward be rewarded by the presidency ; pensions cannot
be made perquisites of party ; the army, *i. e.* the whole
effective force of the nation, will support, and not attempt to subvert, the republic.

The True Social Contract.

The individual enters into social life in Switzerland
with the constitutional guarantee that he shall be independent in all things excepting wherein he has in-
extricable common interests with his fellows.

Each neighborhood aims, as far as possible, to govern itself, so subdividing its functions that even in
these no interference with the individual shall occur

that may be avoided. Adjoining neighborhoods next form a district and as such control certain common interests. Then a greater group, of several districts, unite in the canton. Finally takes place the federation of all the cantons. At each of these necessary steps in organizing society, the avowed intention of the masses concerned is that the primary rights of the individual shall be preserved. Says the "Westminster Review": "The essential characteristic of the federal government is that each of the states which combine to form a union retains in its own hands, in its individual capacity, the management of its own affairs, while authority over matters common to all is exercised by the states in their collective and corporate capacity." And what is thus true of Confederation with respect to the independence of the canton is equally true of canton with respect to the commune, and of the commune with respect to the individual. No departure from home rule, no privileged individuals or corporations, no special legislation, no courts with powers above the people's will, no legal discriminations whatever—such their aim, and in general their successful aim, the Swiss lead all other nations in leaving to the individual his original sovereignty. Wherever this is not the fact, wherever purpose fails fulfillment, the cause lies in long-standing complications which as yet have not yielded to the newer democratic methods. On the side of official organization, one historical abuse after another has been attacked, resulting in the simple, smooth-running, necessary local and national stewardships described. On the side of economic social organization, a concomitant of the political system, the progress in Switzerland has been remarkable. As is to be seen in the following chapter, in the management of natural monopolies the democratic Swiss, beyond any other people, have attained justice, and consequently have distributed much of their increasing wealth with an approach to equity ; while in the system of communal lands practiced in the Landsgemeinde cantons is found an example to land reformers throughout the world.

THE COMMON WEALTH OF SWITZERLAND.

Unless producers may exercise equal right of access to land, the first material for all production, they stand unequal before the law ; and if one man, through legal privilege given to another, is deprived of any part of the product of his labor, justice does not reign. The economic question, then, under any government, relates to legal privilege—to monopoly, either of the land or its products.

With the non-existence of the exclusive enjoyment of monopolies by some men—monopolies in the land, in money-issuing, in common public works—each producer would retain his entire product excepting his taxes. This end secured, there would remain no politico-economic problem excepting that of taxation.

Of recent years the Swiss have had notable success in preventing from falling into private hands certain monopolies that in other countries take from the many to enrich a few. Continuing to act on the principles observed, they must in time establish not only equal rights in the land but the full economic as well as political sovereignty of the individual.

Land and Climate.

Glance at the theatre of the labor of this people. Switzerland, with about 16,000 square miles, equals in

area one-third of New York. Of its territory, 30 per
cent—waterbeds, glaciers, and sterile mountains—is
unproductive. Forests cover 18 per cent. Thus but
half the country is good for crops or pasture. The various altitudes, in which the climate ranges from that
of Virginia to that of Labrador, are divided by agri-
culturists into three zones. The lower zone, including
all lands below a level of 2,500 feet above the sea,
touches, at Lake Maggiore, in the Italian canton of
Ticino, its lowest point, 643 feet above the sea. In this
zone are cultivated wheat, barley, and other grains,
large crops of fruit, and the vine, the latter an abundant source of profit. The second zone, within which
lies the larger part of the country, includes the lower
mountain ranges. Its altitudes are from 2,500 to 5,000
feet, its chief growth great forests of beech, larch,
and pine. Above this rises the Alpine zone, upon the
steep slopes of which are rich pastures, the highest
touching 10,000 feet, though they commonly reach but
8,000, where vegetation becomes sparse and snow and
glaciers begin. In these mountains, a million and a half
cattle, horses, sheep, and goats are fed annually. In
all, Switzerland is not fertile, but rocky, mountainous,
and much of it the greater part of the year snow-covered.

Whatever the individual qualities of the Swiss, their
political arrangements have had a large influence in
promoting the national well-being. This becomes evident with investigation. Observe how they have
placed under public control monopolies that in other
countries breed millionaires :—

Railroads.

One bureau of the Post-Office department exercises federal supervision over the railroads, a second manages the mail and express services, and a third those of the telegraph and telephone.

Of railroads, there are nearly 2,000 miles. Their construction and operation have been left to private enterprise, but from the first the Confederation has asserted a control over them that has stopped short only of management. Hence there are no duplicated lines, no discriminations in rates, no cities at the mercy of railroad corporations, no industries favored by railroad managers and none destroyed. The government prescribes the location of a proposed line, the time within which it must be built, the maximum tariffs for freight and passengers, the minimum number of trains to be run, and the conditions of purchase in case the State at any time should decide to assume possession. Provision is made that when railway earnings exceed a certain ratio to capital invested, the surplus shall be subjected to a proportionately increased tax. Engineers of the Post-Office department superintend the construction and repair of the railroads, and post-office inspectors examine and pass upon the time-tables, tariffs, agreements, and methods of the companies. Hence falsification of reports is prevented, stock watering and exchange gambling are hampered, and "wrecking," as practiced in the United States, is unknown.

Owing to tunnels, cuts, and bridges, the construction of the Swiss railway system has been costly; Mulhall's statistics give Switzerland a higher ratio of railway capital to population than any other country in Europe. Yet the service is cheap, passenger tariffs being considerably less than in France and Great Britain, and, about the same as in Germany, within a shade as low as the lowest in Europe.

Differing from the narrow compartment railway carriages of other European countries, the passenger cars of Switzerland are generally built on the American plan, so that the traveler is enabled to view the scenery ahead, behind, and on both sides. For circular tours, the companies make a reduction of 25 per cent on the regular fare. At the larger stations are interpreters who speak English. Unlike the service in other Continental countries, third class cars are attached to all trains, even the fastest. On the whole, despite the highest railroad investment per head in Europe, Switzerland has the best of railway service at the lowest of rates, the result of centralized State control coupled with free industry under the limitations of that control. In the ripest judgment of the nation up to the present, this system yields better results than any other: by a referendary vote taken in December, 1891, the people refused to change it for State ownership of railroads.

Mails, the Telegraph, the Telephone, and Highways.

The Swiss postal service is a model in completeness, cheapness, and dispatch. Switzerland has 800 post-

offices and 2,000 dépôts where stamps are sold and letters and packages received. Postal cards cost 1 cent;
to foreign countries, 2 cents, and with return flap, 4.
For half-ounce letters, within a circuit of six miles,
the cost is 1 cent; for letters for all Switzerland, up
to half a pound, 2 cents; for printed matter, one
ounce, two-fifths of a cent; to half a pound, 1 cent; one
pound, 2 cents; for samples of goods, to half a pound,
1 cent; one pound, 2 cents.

There are 1,350 telegraph offices open to the public.
A dispatch for any point in Switzerland costs 6 cents
for the stamp and 1 cent for every two words.

The Swiss Post-Office department has many surprises
in store for the American tourist. Mail delivery everywhere free, even in a rural commune remote from the
railroad he may see a postman on his rounds two or
three times a day. When money is sent him by postal
order, the letter-carrier puts the cash in his hands. If
he wishes to send a package by express, the carrier
takes the order, which soon brings to him the postal
express wagon. A package sent him is delivered in
his room. At any post-office he may subscribe for any
Swiss publication or for any of a list of several
thousand of the world's leading periodicals. When
roving in the higher Alps, in regions where the roads
are but bridle paths, the tourist may find in the most
unpretending hotel a telegraph office. If he follows
the wagon roads, he may send his hand baggage ahead
by the stage coach and at the end of his day's walk
find it at his destination.

There are three hundred stage routes in Switzerland, all operated under the Post-Office department, private posting on regular routes being prohibited. The department owns the coaches; contractors own the horses and other material. From most of the termini, at least two coaches arrive and depart daily. Passengers, first and second class, are assigned to seats in the order of purchasing tickets. Every passenger in waiting at a stage office on the departure of a coach must by law be provided with conveyance, several supplementary vehicles often being thus called into employ. A postal coach may be ordered at an hour's notice, even on the mountain routes. Coach fare is 6 cents a mile; in the Alps, 8. Each passenger is allowed thirty-three pounds of baggage; in the Alps, twenty-two. Return tickets are sold at a reduction of 10 per cent.

The cantonal wagon roads of Switzerland are unequaled by any of the highways in America. They are built by engineers, are solidly made, are macadamized, and are kept in excellent repair. The Alpine post roads are mostly cut in or built out upon the steep mountain sides. Not infrequently, they are tunneled through the massive rocky ribs of great peaks. Yet their gradient is so easy that the average tourist walks twenty-five miles over them in a short day. The engineering feats on these roads are in many cases notable. On the Simplon route a wide mountain stream rushes down over a post-road tunnel, and from within the traveler may see through the gallery-like windows the cataract pouring close beside him down into the valley. On the route that passes the great Rhone glacier, the road ascends a high mountain in a zigzag that, as viewed in front from the valley below, looks like a colossal corkscrew. This road is as well kept as. the better turnpikes of New York, teams moving at a fast walk in ascending and at a trot in descending, though the region is barren and uninhabitable, and wintry nine months in the year. These two examples, however, give but a faint idea of the vast number of similar works. The federal treasury appropriates to several of the Alpine cantons, in addition to the sums so expended by the local administrations, from $16,000 to $40,000 a year for the maintenance of their post roads.

With lower postage than any other country, the net earnings of the Swiss postal system for 1889 were $560,000. This, however, is but a fraction of the real gain to the nation from this source. Without their roads, railroads, stage lines, and mail facilities, their hotels, numbering more than one thousand and as a rule excellently managed, could not be maintained for the summer rush of foreign tourists, worth to the country many million dollars a year. The finest Alpine scenery is by no means confined to Swiss boundaries, but within these lines the comforts of travel far surpass those in the neighboring mountainous countries. In Savoy, Lombardy, and the Austrian Tyrol, the traveler must be prepared to put up with comparatively antiquated methods and primitive accommodations.

Yet, previous to 1849, each Swiss canton had its own postal arrangements, some cantons farming out their systems either to other cantons or to individuals. In each canton the service, managed irrespective of federal needs, was costly, and Swiss postal systems, as compared with those of France and Germany, were notoriously behindhand.

Banking.

While the Confederation coins the metallic money current in the country, it is forbidden by the constitution to monopolize the issue of notes or guarantee the circulation of any bank. For the past ten years, however, it has controlled the circulation of the banks, the amount of their reserve fund, and the publication of their reports. The latter may be called for at the discretion of the executive council, in fact even daily.

There are thirty-five banks of issue doing business under cantonal law. Of these, eighteen, known as cantonal banks, either are managed or have their notes guaranteed by the respective cantons. Thus, while banking and money - issuing are free, the cantonal banks insure a requisite note circulation, minimizing the rate of interest and reducing its fluctuations. The setting up of cantonal banks, in order to withdraw privileges from licensed banks, was one of the public questions agitated by social reformers and decided in several of the cantons by direct legislation.

Taxes.

The framework of this little volume does not admit

---

* A vote, October 18, 1891, made note-issuing a federal monopoly.

so much as an outline of the various methods of taxation practiced in Switzerland. As in all countries, they are complex. But certain significant results of direct legislation are to be pointed out. In all the cantons there is a strong tendency to raise revenue from direct, as opposed to indirect, taxes, and from progressive taxation according to fortune. The following, from an editorial in the "Christian Union," February 12, 1891, so justly and briefly puts the facts that I prefer printing it rather than words of my own, which might lie under suspicion of being tinged with the views of a radical : "With the democratic revolution of 1830 the people demanded that direct taxation should be introduced, and since the greater revolution of 1848 they have been steadily replacing the indirect taxes upon necessities by direct taxes upon wealth. In Zurich, for example—where in the first part of this century there were no direct taxes—in 1832 indirect taxation supplied four-fifths of the local revenue ; to-day it supplies but one-seventeenth. The canton raises thirty-two francs per capita by direct taxation where it raises but two by indirect taxation. This change has accompanied the transformation of Switzerland from a nominal to a real democracy. By the use of direct taxation, where every man knows just how much he pays, and by the use of the Referendum, where the sense of justice of the entire public is expressed as to how tax burdens should be distributed, Switzerland has developed a system by which the division of society into the harmfully rich and wretchedly poor has been

checked, if not prevented. In the most advanced cantons, as has been brought out by Professor Cohn in
the 'Political Science Quarterly,' the taxes, both on
incomes and on property, are progressive. In each
case a certain minimum is exempted. In the case of
incomes, the progression is such that the largest incomes pay a rate five times as heavy as the very mod-
erate ones ; while in the case of property, the largest
fortunes pay twice as much as the smallest. The tax
upon inheritances has been most strongly developed.
In the last thirty years it has been increased sixfold.
The larger the amount of property, and the more distant the relative to whom it has been bequeathed,
the heavier the rate is made. It is sometimes as high
as 20 per cent. Speaking upon this point, the New
York 'Evening Post' correspondent says : 'Evidently
there are few countries that do so much to discourage
the accumulation of vast fortunes ; and, in fact, Switzerland has few paupers and few millionaires.'"

Until 1848, each canton imposed cantonal tariff
duties on imported goods, and, as is yet the case in
most continental countries, until a few years ago the
larger cities imposed local import duties (*octrois*). But
the *octroi* is now a thing of the past, and save in one
respect the cantons have abolished cantonal tariffs.
The mining of salt being under federal control, and
the retail price regulated by each canton for itself,
supervision of imports of salt into each canton becomes necessary.

The "Statesmen's Year Book" (1891) gives the debts

of all the cantons of Switzerland as inconsiderable, while the federal debt, in 1890 but eleven million dollars, is less than half the federal assets in stocks and lands. In summing up at the close of his chapter on "State and Local Finance," Prof. Vincent says: "On the whole, the expenditures of Switzerland are much less than those of neighboring states. This may be ascribed in part to the lighter military burden, in part to the fact that no monarchs and courts must be supported, and further, to the inclinations of the Swiss people for practical rather than ornamental matters." And he might pertinently have added, "and to the fact that the citizens themselves hold the public purse-strings."

Limitations to Swiss Freedom.

Certain stumbling blocks stand in the way of sweeping claims as to the freedom enjoyed in Switzerland. One is asked: What as to the suppression of the Jesuits and the Salvation Army? As to the salt and alcohol monopolies of the State? As to the federal protective tariff? What as to the political war two years ago in Ticino?

Two mutually supporting forms of reply are to be made to these queries. One relates to the immediate circumstances under which each of the departures from freedom cited have taken place; the other to historical conditions affecting the development of the Swiss democracy of to-day.

As to the first of these forms of reply:

In the decade previous to 1848 occurred the religious disturbances that ended in the war of the Sonderbund (secession), when several Catholic cantons endeavored to dissolve the loose federal pact under which Switzerland then existed. On the defeat of the secessionists, the movement for a closer federation—for a Confederation—received an impetus, which resulted in the present union. By an article of the constitution then substituted for the pact, convents were abolished and the order of the Jesuits forbidden on Swiss soil. Both had endangered the State. Mild, indeed, is this proscription when compared with the effects of the religious hatreds fostered for centuries between territories now Swiss cantons. In the judgment of the majority this restriction of the freedom of a part is essential to that enjoyed by the nation as a whole.

The exercises of the Salvation Army fell under the laws of the municipalities against nuisances. The final judicial decision in this case was in effect that while persons of every religious belief are free to worship in Switzerland, none in doing so are free seriously to annoy their neighbors.

The present federal protective tariff was imposed just after the federal Referendum (optional) had been called into operation on several other propositions, and, the public mind weary of political agitation, demand for the popular vote on the question was not made. The Geneva correspondent of the Paris "Temps" wrote of the tariff when it was adopted in 1884: "This tariff has sacrificed the interest of the whole of the consumers to temporary coalitions of private interests. It would have been shattered like a card house had it been submitted to the vote of the people." In imposing the tariff, the Federal Assembly in self-defense followed the action of other Continental governments. Many raw materials necessary to manufactures were, however, exempted and the burden of the duties placed on luxuries. As it is, Switzerland, without being able to obtain a pound of cotton except by transit through regions of hostile tariffs, maintains a cotton manufacturing industry holding a place among the foremost of the Continent, while her total trade per head is greater than that of any other country in Europe.

The days of the federal salt monopoly are numbered. The criticisms it has of late evoked portend its end. A popular vote may finish it at any time.

The State monopoly of alcohol, begun in 1887, is as yet an experiment. Financially, it has thus far been moderately successful, though smuggling and other evasions of the law go on on a large scale. The nation, yet in doubt, is awaiting developments. With a reaction, confidently predicted by many, against high tariffs and State interference with trade, the monopoly may be abolished.

The little war in Ticino was the expiring spasm of the ultramontanes, desperately struggling against the advance of the Liberals armed with the Referendum. The reactionaries were suppressed, and the people's law made to prevail. The story, now to be read in the

annual reference books, is a chronicle that cannot fail
to win approval for democracy as an agency of peace
and justice.

The explanations conveyed in these facts imply yet
a deeper cause for the lapses from freedom in question. This cause is that Switzerland, in many cantons
for centuries undemocratic, is not yet entirely democratic. Law cannot rise higher than its source. The
last step in democracy places all lawmaking power
directly and fully in the hands of the majority, but if
by the majority justice is dimly seen, justice will be
imperfectly done. No more may be asserted for democracy than this : (1) That under the domination
of force, at present the common state of mankind, es-
cape from majority rule in some form is impossible. (2)
That hence justice as seen by the majority, exercising
its will in conditions of equality for all, marks the
highest justice obtainable. In their social organization and practice, the Swiss have advanced the line of
justice to where it registers their political,—their mental and moral,—development. Above that, manifestly,
it cannot be carried.

Despite a widespread impression to the contrary, the
traditions for ages of nearly all that now constitutes
Swiss territory have been of tyranny and not of
liberty. In most of that territory, in turn, bishop, king,
noble, oligarch, and politician governed, but until the
past half century, or less, never the masses. Half the
area of Switzerland, at present containing 40 per cent

of the inhabitants, was brought into the federation only in the present century. Of this recent accession, Geneva, for a brief term part of France, had previously long been a pure oligarchy, and more remotely a dictatorship; Neuchâtel had been a dependency of the crown of Prussia, never, in fact, fully released until 1857; Valais and the Grisons, so-called independent confederacies, had been under ecclesiastical rule; Ticino had for three centuries been governed as conquered territory, the privilege of ruling over it purchased by bailiffs from its conquerors, the ancient Swiss League—"a harsh government," declares the Encyclopædia Britannica, "one of the darkest passages of Swiss history." Of the older Switzerland, Bâle, Berne, and Zurich were oligarchical cities, each holding in feudality extensive neighboring regions. Not until 1833 were the peasants of Bâle placed on an equal footing with the townspeople, and then only after serious disturbances. And the inequalities between lord and serf, victor and vanquished, voter and disfranchised, existed in all the older states save those now known as the Landsgemeinde cantons. Says Vincent: "Almost the only thread that held the Swiss federation together was the possession of subject lands. In these they were interested as partners in a business corporation. Here were revenues and offices to watch and profits to divide, and matters came to such a pass that almost the only questions upon which the Diet could act in concert were the inspection of accounts and other affairs connected with the subject territories. The common properties were all that prevented complete rupture on several critical occasions. Another marked feature in the condition of government was the supremacy gained by the patrician class. Municipalities gained the upper hand over rural districts, and within the municipalities the old families assumed more and more privileges in government, in society, and in trade. The civil service in some instances became the monopoly of a limited number of families, who were careful to perpetuate all their privileges. Even in the rural democracies there was more or less of this family supremacy visible. Sporadic attempts at reform were rigorously suppressed in the cities, and government became more and more petrified into aristocracy. A study of this period of Swiss history explains many of the provisions found in the constitutions of today, which seem like over-precaution against family influence. The effect of privilege was especially grievous, and the fear of it survived when the modern constitutions were made."

Here, plainly, are the final explanations of any shortcomings in Swiss liberty. In those parts of Switzerland where these shortcomings are serious, modern ideas of equality in freedom have not yet gained ascendency over the ages-honored institution of inequality. Progress is evident, but the goal of possible freedom is yet distant. How, indeed, could it be otherwise when in several cantons it was only in 1848, with the Confederation, that manhood suffrage was established?

But how, it may be inquired, did the name of Swiss ever become the synonym of liberty? This land whose soldiery hired out as mercenaries to foreign princes, this League of oppressors, this hotbed of religious conflicts and persecutions,—how came it to be regarded as the home of a free people!

The truth is that the traditional reputation of the whole country is based on the ancient character of a part. The Landsgemeinde cantons alone bear the test of democratic principles. Within them, indeed, for a thousand years the two primary essentials of democracy have prevailed. They are:

(1) That the entire citizenship vote the law.

(2) That land is not property, and its sole just tenure is occupancy and use.

The first-named essential is yet in these cantons fully realized; largely, also, is the second.

The Communal Lands of Switzerland.

As to the tenure of the land held in Switzerland as private property, Hon. Boyd Winchester, for four years American minister at Berne, in his recent work, "The Swiss Republic," says: "There is no country in Europe where land possesses the great independence, and where there is so wide a distribution of land ownership as in Switzerland. The 5,378,122 acres devoted to agriculture are divided among 258,637 proprietors, the average size of the farms throughout the whole country being not more than twenty-one acres. The facilities for the acquisition of land have produced small holders, with security of tenure, representing two-thirds the entire population. There are no primogeniture, copyhold, customary tenure, and manorial rights, or other artificial obstacles to discourage land transfer and dispersion." "There is no belief in Switzerland that land was made to administer to the perpetual elevation of a privileged class ; but a widespread and positive sentiment, as Turgot puts it, that 'the earth belongs to the living and not to the dead,' nor, it may be added, to the unborn."

Turgot's dictum, however, obtains no more than to this extent : (1) The cantonal testamentary laws almost invariably prescribe division of property among all the children—as in the code Napoleon, which prevails in French Switzerland, and which permits the testator to dispose of only a third of his property, the rest being divided among all the heirs. (2) Highways, including the railways, are under immediate government control. (3) The greater part of the forests are managed, much of them owned, by the Confederation. (4) In nearly all the communes, some lands, often considerable in area, are under communal administration. (5) In the Landsgemeinde cantons largely, and in other cantons in a measure, inheritance and participation, jointly and severally, in the communal lands are had by the members of the communal corporation—that is, by those citizens who have acquired rights in the public property of the commune.

Nearly every commune in Switzerland has public lands. In many communes, where they are mostly

wooded, they are entirely in charge of the local government ; in others, they are in part leased to individuals ; in others, much of them is worked in common
by the citizens having the right ; but in the Landsgemeinde cantons it is customary to divide them period-
ically among the members of the corporation.

Of the Landsgemeinde cantons, one or two yet have
nearly as great an area of public land as of private.
The canton of Uri has nearly 1,000 acres of cultivated
lands, the distribution of which gives about a quarter
of an acre to each family entitled to a share. Uri has
also forest lands worth between 4,000,000 and 5,000,000
francs, representing a capital of nearly 1,500 francs to
each family. The commune of Obwald, in Unterwald,
with 13,000 inhabitants, has lands and forests valued
at 11,350,000 francs. Inner Rhodes, in Appenzell, with
12,000 inhabitants, has land valued at 3,000,000 francs.
Glarus, because of its manufactures, is one of the richest cantons in public domain. In the non-Landsgemeinde German cantons, there is much common land.
One-third of all the lands of the canton of Schaffhausen is held by the communes. The town of Soleure
has forests, pastures, and cultivated lands worth about
6,000,000 francs. To the same value amounts the common property of the town of St. Gall. In the canton
of St. Gall the communal Alpine pasturages comprise
one-half such lands. Schwyz has a stretch of common
land (an *allmend*) thirty miles in length and ten to fifteen in breadth. The city of Zurich has a well-kept
forest of twelve to fifteen square miles, worth millions

of francs.   Winterthur, the second town in Zurich, has
so many forests and vineyards that for a long period
its citizens not only had no taxes to pay, but every autumn each received gratis several cords of wood and
many gallons of wine.   Numerous small towns and villages in German Switzerland collect no local taxes,
and give each citizen an abundance of fuel.   In addition to free fuel, cultivable lands are not infrequently
allotted.   At Stanz, in Unterwald, every member of the
corporation is given more than an acre.   At Buchs, in
St. Gall, each member receives more than an acre, with
firewood and grazing ground for several head of cattle.
Upward of two hundred French communes possess
common lands.   In the canton of Vaud, a number of
the communes have large revenues in wood and butter from the forests and pastures of the Jura mountains.   Geneva has great forests ; Valais many vineyards.

In the canton of Valais, communal vineyards and
grain fields are cultivated in common.   Every member
of the corporation who would share in the produce of
the land contributes a certain share of work in field
or vineyard.   Part of the revenue thus obtained
is expended in the purchase of cheese.   The rest of
the yield provides banquets in which all the members take part.

Excepting in the case of forests, the trend is away
from working the lands in common.   Examples of the
later methods are to be seen in the cantons of Ticino
and Glarus, as follows :—

Several communes in Ticino, notably Airolo, have much public wealth. Airolo has seventeen mountain pastures, each of which feeds forty to eighty head of cattle. Each member of the corporation has the right to send up to these pastures five head for the summer. Those sending more, pay for the privilege ; those sending less, receive a rental. On a specified day at the beginning of the season and on another at the close, the milk of each cow is weighed ; from these amounts her average yield is estimated, and her total produce computed. The cheese and butter from the herds are sold, most of it in Milan, the hire of the herders paid, and the net revenue divided among the members according to the yield of their cows.

In Glarus, the produce of the greater part of the communal lands, instead of being directly divided among the inhabitants, is substituted for taxation. The commonable alps are let by auction for a term of years, and, in opposition to ancient principles, strangers may bid for them. Some of the Glarus communes sell the right to cut timber in the forest under the superintendence of the guardians. The mountain hotels, in not a few instances the property of the communes, are let year by year. Land is frequently rented from the communes by manufacturing establishments. A citizen not using his share of the communal land may lease it to the commune, which in turn will let it to a tenant. The communes of Glarus are watchful that enough arable land is preserved for distribution among the members. If a plot is sold to manu-

facturers, or for private building purposes, a piece of
equal or greater extent is bought elsewhere. Glarus
has relatively as many people engaged in industries
aside from farming as any other spot in Europe. It
has 34,000 inhabitants, of whom nearly 15,000 live directly by manufactures, while of the rest many indirectly receive something from the same source. Dis-
tributive coöperative societies on the English plan
exist in most of the industrial communes. The members of the communal corporations in Glarus, though
not rich, are as free and independent as any other
wage-workers in the world : they inherit the common
lands ; their local taxes are little or nothing ; they are
assured work, if not in the manufactories then on the
land.

Of the poverty that fears pauperism in old age, that
dreads enforced idleness in recurrent industrial crises,
that undermines health, that sinks human beings in ig-
norance, that deprives men of their manhood, the Swiss
who enjoy the common lands of the Landsgemeinde
cantons know little or nothing. They have enough.
They have nothing to waste, nothing to spare ; their
fare is simple. But they are free. It is to the like
freedom and equality of their ancestors that histori-
ans have pointed. It would be well nigh meaningless
to refer to any freedom and equality among other
ancient Swiss. The right of asylum from religious
oppression is the sole feature of liberty at all general
of old. The present is the first generation in which
all the Swiss have been free. The chief elements of

their political freedom—the Initiative and Referendum—came from the Landsgemeinde cantons. From the same source, in good time, so also may come to all Switzerland the prime element of economic freedom—free access to land.

Poverty is a relative condition. Men may be poor of mind—ignorant; and of body—ill-fed, ill-clothed, ill-sheltered; and of rights—dependent. And from the state of hopeless deprivation involving all these forms upward are minute gradations. Where stand the Swiss in the scale?

This the reply : Their system of education gives free opportunity to all to partake of the mental heritage of the ages. Their method of distribution, through the inheritance laws, of private and common lands, has made roughly two-thirds of the heads of families agricultural land holders. There being in other regards government control of all monopolies, the consequence is a widespread distribution of the annual product. Hence, no pauperism to be compared with that of England ; no plutocracy such as we have in America. Certain other facts broadly outline the general comfort and independence. As one effect of the subdivision of the land, the soil, so far as nature permits, is highly cultivated, its appearance fertile, finished, beautiful, and in striking contrast with the dominating vast, bare mountain rocks and snowbeds. The many towns and cities bear abundant signs of a general prosperity, their roads, bridges, stores, residences,

and public buildings betokening in the inhabitants
industry and energy, and freedom to employ these
qualities. Emigration is at low percentage, and of
those citizens who do leave for the New World not a
few are educated persons with some means seeking
short cuts to fortune. Much of the rough work of
Switzerland is done by Savoyards, as houseworkers,
and by Italians, as farm hands, laborers, and stone ma-
sons : showing that as a body even the poorest of the
propertyless Swiss have some choice of the better paid occupations. Every spring sees Italians,
by scores of thousands, pouring over the Alps for
a summer's work in Switzerland. Indeed, Swiss wage-
workers might command better terms were it not
for competing Italians, French, and Germans. In other
words, through just social arrangements, enough has
been done in Switzerland to raise the economic level
of the entire nation ; but the overflow of laborers from
other lands depresses the condition of home labor.
Nevertheless, where, it may be asked, is the people
higher in the scale of civilization, in all the word im-
plies, than the Swiss ?

To recount what the Swiss have done by direct
legislation :

They have made it easy at any time to alter their
cantonal and federal constitutions,—that is, to change,
even radically, the organization of society, the social
contract, and thus to permit a peaceful revolution at
the will of the majority. They have as well cleared

from the way of majority rule every obstacle,—privilege of ruler, fetter of ancient law, power of legislator. They have simplified the structure of government, held their officials as servants, rendered bureaucracy impossible, converted their representatives to simple committeemen, and shown the parliamentary system not essential to lawmaking. They have written their laws in language so plain that a layman may be judge in the highest court. They have forestalled monopolies, improved and reduced taxation, avoided incurring heavy public debts, and made a better distribution of their land than any other European country. They have practically given home rule in local affairs to every community. They have calmed disturbing political elements ;—the press is purified, the politician disarmed, the civil service well regulated. Hurtful partisanship is passing away. Since the people as a whole will never willingly surrender their sovereignty, reactionary movement is possible only in case the nation should go backward. But the way is open forward. Social ideals may be realized in act and institution. Even now the liberty-loving Swiss citizen can discern in the future a freedom in which every individual,—independent, possessed of rights in nature's resources and in command of the fruits of his toil,—may, at his will, on the sole condition that he respect the like aim of other men, pursue his happiness.

DIRECT LEGISLATION IN THE UNITED STATES.

" But these are foreign methods. How are they to be engrafted on our American system?" More than once have I been asked this question when describing the Initiative and Referendum of Switzerland.

The reply is : Direct legislation is not foreign to this country. Since the settlement of New England its practice has been customary in the town meeting, an institution now gradually spreading throughout the western states—of recent years with increased rapidity. The Referendum has appeared, likewise, with respect to state laws, in several forms in every part of the Union. In the field of labor organization, also, especially in several of the more carefully managed national unions, direct legislation is freely practiced. The institution does not need to be engrafted on this republic ; it is here ; it has but to develop naturally.

The Town Meeting.

The town meeting of New England is the counterpart of the Swiss communal political meeting. Both assemblies are the primary form of the politico-social organization. Both are the foundation of the structure of the State. The essential objects of both are the same : to enact local regulations, to elect local officers, to fix local taxation, and to make appropriations for local purposes. At both, any citizen may propose measures, and these the majority may accept or reject —*i. e.*, the working principles of town and commune alike are the Initiative and the Referendum.

A fair idea of the proceedings at all town meetings may be gained through description of one. For several reasons, a detailed account here of what actually happened recently at a town meeting is, it seems to me, justified. At such a gathering is seen, in plain operation, in the primary political assembly, the principles of direct legislation. The departure from those principles in a representative gathering is then the more clearly seen. In many parts of the country, too, the methods of the town meeting are little known. By observing the transactions in particular, the reader will learn the variety in the play of democratic principle and draw from it instructive inference.

The town of Rockland, Plymouth county, in the east of Massachusetts, has 5,200 inhabitants ; assesses for taxation 5,787 acres of land ; contains 1,078 dwelling houses, 800 of which are occupied by owners, and numbers 1,591 poll tax payers, who are therefore voters.

At 9 a. m., on Monday, March 2, 1891, 819 voters of Rockland assembled in the opera house for the annual town meeting, the "warrant" for which, in accordance with the law, had been publicly posted seven days before and published once in each of the two town newspapers. A presiding officer for the day, called a moderator, was elected by show of hands, after which an election by ballot for town officers for the ensuing year was begun. The supervisors of the voting were the town clerk and the three selectmen (the executive officers of the town), who were seated on a platform at one end of the hall. To cast his ballot, a voter mounted the platform, his name was called aloud by the clerk, his ballot was deposited, a check bell striking as it was thrown in the ballot-box, and the voter stepped on and down. The ballot was a printed one, its size, color, and type regulated by state law. When the voters had cast their ballots, five tellers, who had been chosen by show of hands, counted the vote. In this balloting for town officers, there was no division into Republicans and Democrats, although considerable grouping together through party association could be traced. The officers elected were a town clerk and treasurer ; a board of three, to serve as selectmen, assessors, overseers of the poor, and fence viewers ; three school committeemen ; a water commissioner ; a board of health of three members ; two library trustees ; three auditors, and seven constables.

A vote was also taken by ballot—" Yes " or " No "—on the question : " Shall licenses be granted for the sale of intoxicating liquors in this town ?" The yeas were 317 ; nays, 347. The form of ballot used in this case was precisely that invariably employed in the Referendum in Switzerland.

After a recess of an hour at midday, the business laid out in the " warrant " was resumed. There were present 700 to 800 voters, with, as on-lookers on the same floor, a large number of women, the principal and pupils of the high school, and the teachers and children of the grammar schools.

The "warrant" (the schedule for the meeting) consisted of forty-four "articles," each representing a matter to be debated and voted on—that is to say, a subject for legislation.   These articles had been placed in the warrant by the selectmen, either on their own motion or on request of citizens.   The election of moderator had taken place under article 1 ; that of town officers under article 2 ; the license vote under article 3.   The voting on the rest of the articles now took place by show of hands.   Article 4 related to the annual reports of the town officers, printed copies of which were to be had by each citizen.   These were read and discussed. Article 5 related to the general appropriations for town expenses for the ensuing year.   The following were decided on, each item being voted on separately :

For highway repairs - -	$3,800	For military aid - - - - $500
For removing snow - -	300	For guideboards - - - 50
For fire department - -	1,200	For abatement of taxes and
For police service - - -	500	collector's fee - - - 500
For night watch - - -	600	For support of poor - - 5,500
For town officers - - -	2,200	For library, etc - - - - 1,000
For town committees, and		For schools, proper - - 11,300
Abingdon records -	50	For school-incidentals - 1,000
For miscellaneous expenses	1,200	For school books - - - 1,000
For interest - - - -	1,000	For hydrants - - - - 2,300
For memorial day - -	100	For water bonds, etc - 2,500

Article 6, which was agreed to, authorized the town treasurer to borrow money in anticipation of the collection of taxes; article 7 related to the method of collecting the town taxes. It was decided these should be farmed out to the lowest bidder, and, on the spot, a citizen secured the contract at sixty-eight cents on the hundred. Article 8 related to the powers of the tax collector ; 9, to a list of jurors reported by the selectmen, which was accepted ; 10, to methods of repairing highways and sidewalks ; 11, to appropriating money for memorial day. Articles 10 and 11 were passed over, having been covered in the general appropriations, and the selectmen were instructed to enforce in highway work the nine-hour law. Article 12, which was adopted, provided for a night watch ; 13, relating to copying the records of Abingdon, had been passed upon in the general appropriations ; 14, providing for widening and straightening a street, was passed, and $350 appropriated for the purpose ; 15, providing for concrete sidewalks, excited much debate, and $300 was appropriated in addition to material on hand. Articles 16, appropriating $350 for draining a street, and 17, requesting the selectmen to lay out a water course on another street, were adopted. Article 18, which was carried by a large majority, appropriated, in five items, discussed and voted on separately, $7,250 for the fire department. Article 19 appropriated $100 for a town road, 20 $200 for another, and these were adopted, but 21, by which $325 was asked for another road, was laid on the table. Articles 22 and 23, appropriating $75 and $25 for bridges, were passed. Article 24, proposing the graveling of a sidewalk, was referred to the selectmen. Articles 25, 26, 27, and 28, proposing the laying of sidewalks, were adopted, with appropriations of $150, $125, $150, and $150 ; but 29, also proposing a new sidewalk, was laid on the table. Article 30, proposing a new sidewalk, was adopted, with an appropriation of $300, but 31, proposing another, was laid on the table. Articles 32, proposing to change the grading of two streets, with an appropriation of $500 ; 33, appropriating $300 for a highway roller ; 34, providing for a public drinking fountain, and appropriating $200 ; 35, providing for a new bridge, and appropriating $75, were all adopted. Articles 36, 37, and 38, providing for extensions to the water mains, were laid on the table. Article 39, appropriating $300 for relocation of a telephone line, was adopted ; but articles 40, providing for a memorial building, 41, providing for a town hall, and 42, providing for a soldiers' memorial, were laid on the table. Lastly, articles 43 and 44, providing for changes in street names, were accepted as reported by the selectmen.

After finishing the "warrant," the meeting appropriated $10 to pay the moderator, fixed $3 a day as the rate for the selectmen, and directed the latter not to employ as constable any man who had been rejected by a vote of the town. It was 10.45 p. m. when the assemblage broke up, a recess having been taken from 5.30 to 7.30.

The proceedings at this meeting were characterized by democratic methods. When the town officers handed in their reports, they were questioned and criticised by one citizen and another. A motion to refer the general appropriation list to a committee of twenty-five met with overwhelming defeat in the face of the expressed sentiment that about all left of primitive democracy was the old-fashioned town meeting. One of the speakers on the town library appropriation was a lady, and her point was carried. On the question of buying new fire extinguishing apparatus, there were sides and leaders, with prolonged debate. As to roads and bridges, each matter was dealt with on its own merits and separately from other similar propositions. In the election for officers, women voted for school committeemen.

The only officials of Rockland under annual salary are the treasurer and town physician. Selectmen receive a sum per diem; constables, fees; school committeemen make out their own bills. The others serve for nothing.

Rockland, politically, is a typical New England town. What is to be said of its manner of town meeting may, with little modification, be said of all. Each citizen present at such a meeting may join in the debate. From the printed copy of the officers' reports he may learn what his town government has done in the year past; from the printed warrant he may see what is proposed to be done in the year coming. He who knows the better way in any of the business is sure to receive a hearing. The pockets of all being concerned, whatever is best and cheapest is insured. Bribery, successful only in the dark, has little or no field in the town meeting.

Provision usually exists by which a town may dispose of any urgent matters springing up for legislation in the course of the year : as a rule a special town meeting may be called on petition of a small number of citizens, commonly seven to eleven.

In a study of the town meeting system of today, in "Harper's Monthly," June, 1891, Henry Loomis Nelson brought out many convincing facts as to its superiority over government by a town board. Where the cost for public lighting in a New England town had been but $2,000, in a New York town of the same size it had amounted to $11,000. The cities of Worcester, Mass., and Syracuse, New York, each of about 80,000 inhabitants, were compared, with the New England city in every respect by far the more economically governed. Towns in New England are uniformly superior to others in other parts of the country with regard to the extent of sewers and paved streets. The aggregate of town debts in New England is vastly less than the aggregate for a similar population in the Middle States. The state constitutions of New England commonly relate to fundamental principles, since each district may protect itself by the town meeting ; but outside New England, to assert the rights of localities, state constitutions usually perforce embody particulars. In their fire and police departments, and public school and water supply systems, New England towns lead the rest of the country. " The influence," says Mr. Nelson, " of the town meeting government upon the physical character of the country, upon the highways and bridges, and upon the appearance of the villages, is familiar to all who have traveled through New England. The excellent roads, the stanch bridges, the trim tree-shaded streets, the universal signs of thrift and of the people's pride in the outward aspects of their villages, are too well known to be dwelt upon." In every New England community many of the men are qualified by experience to take charge of a public meeting and conduct its proceedings with some regard to the forms observed in parliamentary bodies. But elsewhere in the Union few of the citizens have any knowledge of such forms and observances. " In New England there is not a voter who may not, and very few voters who do not, actively participate in the work of government. In the other parts of the country hardly any one takes part in public affairs except the office-holder."

John Fiske, in " Civil Government in the United States," (1890), says that " the general tendency toward the spread of township government in the more recently settled parts of the United States is unmistakable." The first western state to adopt the town meeting system was Michigan ; but it now prevails in four-fifths of the counties of Illinois ; in one-sixth of Missouri, where it was begun in 1879 ; and in one-third of the counties of Nebraska, which adopted it in 1883 ; while it has gone much further in Minnesota and Dakota, in which states it has been law since 1878 and 1883, respectively.

"Within its proper sphere," says Fiske, "government by town meeting is the form of government most effectively under watch and control. Everything is done in the full daylight of publicity. The specific objects for which public money is to be appropriated are discussed in the presence of everybody, and any one who disapproves of any of these objects, or of the way in which it is proposed to obtain it, has an opportunity to declare his opinions." "The inhabitant of a New England town is perpetually reminded that 'our government' is 'the people.' Although he may think loosely about the government of his state or the still more remote government at Washington, he is kept pretty close to the facts where local affairs are concerned, and in this there is a political training of no small value."

The same writer notes in the New England towns a tendency to retain good men in office, such as we have seen is the case in Switzerland. "The annual election affords an easy means of dropping an unsatisfactory officer. But in practice nothing has been more common than for the same persons to be re-elected as selectmen or constables or town-clerks for year after year, as long as they are willing or able to serve. The notion that there is anything peculiarly American or democratic in what is known as 'rotation in office' is therefore not sustained by the practice of the New England town, which is the most complete democracy in the world." In another feature is there resemblance to Swiss custom: some of the town officials serve without pay and none receive exorbitant salaries.

The Referendum in States, Cities, Counties, Etc.

Few are aware of the advances which direct legislation has made in state government in the United States. Many facts on this subject, collected by Mr. Ellis P. Oberholtzer, were published in the "Annals of the American Academy of Political and Social Science," November, 1891. Condensed, this writer's statement is as follows : Constitutional amendments now go to the people for a vote in every state except Delaware. The significance of this fact, and the resemblance of this vote to the Swiss Referendum, are seen when one considers the subject matter of a state constitution. Nowadays, such a constitution usually limits a legislature to a short biennial session and defines in detail what laws the legislature may and may not pass. In fact, then, in adopting a constitution once in ten or twenty years, the voters of a state decide upon admissible legislation. Thus they themselves are the real legislators. Among the matters once left entirely to legislatures, but now commonly dealt with in constitutions, are the following : Prohibiting or regulating the liquor traffic ; prohibiting or chartering lotteries ; determining tax rates ; founding and locating state schools and other state institutions ; establishing a legal rate of interest; fixing the salaries of public officials ; drawing up railroad and other corporation regulations ; and defining the relations of husbands and wives, and of debtors and creditors. In line with all this is a tendency to easy amendment. In nearly all the new states and in those older ones which have recently revised their constitutions, the time in which amendments may be effected is as a rule but half of that formerly required. Where once the approval of two successive legislatures was exacted, now the consent of one is considered sufficient.

In fifteen states, until submitted to a popular vote, no law changing the location of the capital is valid ; in seven, no laws establishing banking corporations ; in eleven, no laws for the incurrence of debts excepting such as are specified in the constitution, and no excess of "casual deficits" beyond a stipulated sum ; in several, no rate of assessment exceeding a figure proportionate to the aggregate valuation of the taxable property. Without the Referendum, Illinois cannot sell its state canal ; Minnesota cannot pay interest or principal of the Minnesota railroad ; North Carolina cannot extend the state credit to aid any person or corporation, excepting to help certain railroads unfinished in 1876. With the Referendum, Colorado may adopt woman suffrage and create a debt for public buildings; Texas may fix a location for a college for colored youth ; Wyoming may decide on the sites for its state university, insane asylum and penitentiary.

Numerous important examples of the Referendum in local matters in the United States, especially in the West, were found by Mr. Oberholtzer. There are many county, city, township, and school district referendums. Nineteen state constitutions guarantee to counties the right to fix by vote of the citizens the location of the county seats. So also usually of county lines, divisions of counties, and like matters. Several western states leave it to a vote of the counties as to when they shall adopt a township organization, with town meetings ; several states permit their cities to decide when they shall also be counties. As in the state, there are debt and tax matters that may be passed on only by the people of cities, boroughs, counties, or school districts. Without the Referendum, no municipality in Pennsylvania may contract an aggregate debt beyond 2 per cent of the assessed valuation of its taxable property ; no municipalities in certain other states may incur in any year an indebtedness beyond their revenues ; no local governments in the new states of the West may raise any loans whatever ; none in other states may exceed certain limits in tax rates. With the Referendum, certain Southern communities may make harbor improvements, and other communities may extend the local credit to railroad, water transportation, and similar corporations. The prohibition of the liquor business in a city or county is often left to a popular vote ; indeed, "local option" is the commonest form of Referendum. In California any city with more than 10,000 inhabitants may frame a charter for its own government, which, however, must be approved by the legislature. Under this law Stockton, San José, Los Angeles, and Oakland have acquired new charters. In the state of Washington, cities of 20,000 may make their own charters without the legislature having any power of veto. Largely, then, such cities make their own laws.

In fact, the vast United States seems to have seen as much of the Referendum as little Switzerland. But the effect of the practice has been largely lost in the great size of this country and in the loose and unsystematized character of the institution as known here.

In the "American Commonwealth" of James Bryce, a member of Parliament, there is a chapter entitled "Direct Legislation by the People." After reciting many facts similar in character to those given by Mr. Oberholtzer, Mr. Bryce inquires into the practical workings of direct legislation. He finds what are to his mind some "obvious demerits." Of these demerits, such as apply to details he develops in the course of his statements of several cases of Referendum. In summing up, he further points out what seem to him two objections to the principle. One is that direct legislation "tends to lower the authority and sense of responsibility of the legislature." But this is precisely the aim of pure democracy, and from its point of view a merit of the first order. The other objection is, "it refers matters needing much elucidation by debate to the determination of those who cannot, on account of their numbers, meet together for discussion, and many of whom may have never thought about the matter." But why meet together for discussion? Mr. Bryce here overlooks that this is the age of newspaper and telegraph, and that through these sources the facts and much debate on any matter of public interest may be forthcoming on demand. Mr. Bryce, however, sees more advantages than demerits in direct legislation. Of the advantages he remarks: "The improvement of the legislatures is just what the Americans despair of, or, as they would prefer to say, have not time to attend to. Hence they fall back on the Referendum as the best course available under the circumstances of the case and in such a world as the present. They do not claim that it has any great educative effect on the people. But they remark with truth that the mass of the people are equal in intelligence and character to the average state legislator, and are exposed to fewer temptations. The legislator can be 'got at,' the people cannot. The personal interest of the individual legislator in passing a measure for chartering banks or spending the internal improvement fund may be greater than his interest as one of the community in preventing bad laws. It will be otherwise with the bulk of the citizens. The legislator may be subjected by the advocates of women's suffrage or liquor prohibition to a pressure irresistible by ordinary mortals; but the citizens are too numerous to be all wheedled or threatened. Hence they can and do reject proposals which the legislature has assented to. Nor should it be forgotten that in a country where law depends for its force on the consent of the governed, it is eminently desirable that law should not outrun popular sentiment, but have the whole weight of the people's deliverance behind it."

The Initiative and Referendum in Labor Organizations.

The Referendum is well known to the Knights of Labor. For nine years past expressions of opinion have been asked of the local assemblies by the general executive board. The recent decision of the order to enter upon independent political action was made by a vote in response to a circular issued by the General Master Workman. The latter, at the annual convention at Toledo, in November, 1891, recommended that the Referendum form a part of the government machinery throughout the United States. The Knights being in some respects a secret organization, data as to referendary votings are not always made public.

For the past decade or longer several of the national and international trades-unions of America have had the Initiative and Referendum in operation. Within the past five years the institution in various forms has been taken up by other unions, and at present it is in more or less practice in the following bodies, all associated with the American Federation of Labor :

National or International Union.	No. of Local Unions.	No. of Members, December, 1891.
Journeymen Bakers	81	17,500
Brewery Workmen	61	9,500
United Broth'h'd of Carpenters and Joiners	740	65,000
Amalgamated Carpenters and Joiners	40	2,800
Cigar-Makers	310	27,000
Carriage and Wagon Makers	11	2,000
Garment Workers	24	4,000
Granite Cutters	75	20,000
Tailors	170	17,000
Typographical Union	290	28,000
Total		192,800

Direct legislation has long been familiar to the members of the International Cigar-Makers' Union. Today, amendments to its constitution, the acts of its executives, and even the resolutions passed at delegate conventions, are submitted to a vote by ballot in the local unions. The nineteenth annual convention, held at Indianapolis, September, 1891, provisionally adopted 114 amendments to the constitution and 33 resolutions on various matters. Though some of the latter were plainly perfunctory in character, all of these 147 propositions were printed in full in the "Official Journal" for October, and voted on in the 310 unions throughout America in November. The Initiative is introduced in this international union through local unions. When twenty of the latter have passed favorably on a measure, it must be submitted to the entire body. An idea of the financial transactions of the Cigar-Makers' International Union may be gathered from its total expenditures in the past twelve years and a half. In all, it has disbursed in that time $1,426,208. Strikes took $469,158; sick benefits, $439,010; death benefits, $109,608; traveling benefits, $372,455, and out of work benefits, $35,795. The advance of the Referendum in this great union has been very gradual. It began in 1877 with voting on constitutional amendments. The most recent, and perhaps last possible, step was to transfer the election of the general executive board from the annual convention to the entire body.

The United Garment Workers of America practice

direct legislation under Article 24 of their constitution, which is printed under the caption,"Referendum and Initiative." It prescribes two methods of Initiative. One is that three or more local unions, if of different states, may instruct the general secretary to call for a referendary vote in the unions of the national organization. The other is that the general executive board must so submit all questions of general importance. The general secretary issues the call within two weeks after the petition for a vote reaches him, and the vote is taken within six months afterward. Eighteen propositions passed by the annual convention of this union at Boston, in November, 1891, were submitted to a vote of the local unions in December.

In 1890, the local unions of the International Typographical Union, then numbering nearly 290, voted on twenty-five propositions submitted from the annual convention. In 1891, fourteen propositions were submitted. Of the latter, one authorized the formation of unions of editors and reporters ; another directed the payments to the President to be a salary of $1,400, actual railroad fares by the shortest possible routes, and $3 a day for hotel expenses ; another rescinded a six months' exemption from a per capita tax for newly formed unions ; another provided for a funeral benefit of $50 on the death of a member ; by another an assessment of ten cents a month was levied for the home for superannuated and disabled union printers. All fourteen were adopted, the majorities, however, varying from 558 to 8,758.

Is Complete Direct Legislation in Government Practicable?

The conservative citizen, contented with the existing state of things, is wont to brush aside proposed innovations in government. To do so he avails himself of a familiar stock of objections. But have they not all their answer in the facts thus far brought forth in these chapters? Will he entertain no "crazy theories"? Here is offered practice, proven in varied and innumerable tests to be thoroughly feasible. He is opposed to foreign institutions? Here is a time-honored American institution. He holds that men cannot be made better by law? Here are facts to show that with change of law justice has been promoted. He deems democracy feebleness? Here has been shown its stalwart strength. He is sure workingmen are incapable of managing large affairs? Let him look to the cigarmakers—their capacity for organization, their self-restraint as an industrial army, the soundness of their financial system, the mastery of their employers in the eight-hour question. He believes the intricacies of taxation and estimates of appropriation beyond the average mind? He may see a New England town meeting in a single day dispose of scores of items and, with each settled to a nicety, vote away fifty thousand dollars. He fears state legislation, by reason of its complexity, would prove a puzzle to the ordinary voter? Why, then, are the more vexatious subjects so often shifted by the legislators to the people?

The conservative objector is, first, apt to object before fully examining what he dissents from, and, secondly, prone to have in mind ideal conditions with which to compare the new methods commended to him. In the matter of legislation, he dreams of a body of high-minded lawgivers, just, wise, unselfish, and not of legislators as they commonly are. He forgets that Congress and the legislatures have each a permanent lobby, buying privileges for corporations, and otherwise influencing and corrupting members. He forgets the party caucus, at which the individual member is swamped in the majority; the "strikers," members employing their powers in blackmail; the Black Horse Cavalry, a combination of members in state legislatures formed to enrich themselves by plunder through passing or killing bills. He forgets the scandalous jobs put through to reward political workers; the long lists of doubtful or vicious bills reviewed in the press after each session of every legislative body; the pamphlets issued by reform bodies in which perhaps three-fourths of a legislature is named as untrustworthy, and the price of many of the members given. The City Reform Club of New York published in 1887: "As with the city's repesentatives of 1886, the chief objects of most of the New York members were to make money in the 'legislative business,' to advance their own political fortunes, and to promote the interests of their factions." And where is the state legislature of which much the same things cannot be said?

The conservative objector may not know how the most important bills are often passed in Congress.

He may not know that until toward the close of a session the business of Congress is political in the party
sense rather than in the governing sense ; that on the
floor the play is usually conducted for effect on
the public ; that in committees, measures into which
politics enter are made up either on compromise or
for partisan purposes ; that, finally, in the last days of
a session, the work of legislation is a scramble. The
second day before the adjournment of the last Congress was thus described in a New York daily paper:
" Congress has been working like a gigantic thresh-
ing machine all day long, and at this hour there is
every prospect of an all-night session of both houses.
Helter-skelter, pell-mell, the 'unfinished business' has
been poured into the big hopper, and in less time than
it takes to tell it, it has come out at the other end com-
pleted legislation, lacking only the President's signa-
ture to fit it for the statute books. Public bills providing for the necessary expenses of the government,
private bills galore having as their beneficiaries favored individuals, jobbery in the way of unnecessary
public buildings, railroad charters, and bridge construction—all have been rushed through at lightning
speed, and the end is not yet. A majority of the House
members, desperate because their power and influence
terminate with the end of this brief session, and a
partisan Speaker, whose autocratic rule will prevail
but thirty-six short hours longer, have left nothing
unattempted whereby party friends and protégés
might be benefited. It is safe to say that aside from a

half dozen measures of real importance and genuine merit the country would be no worse off should every other bill not yet acted upon fail of passage. Certain it is that large sums of money would be saved to the Government." And what observer does not know that scenes not unlike this are repeated in almost every legislature in its closing hours?

As between such manner of even national legislation on the one hand, and on the other the entire citizenship voting (as soon would be the fact under direct legislation) on but what properly should be law—and on principles, on policies, and on aggregates in appropriations—would there be reason for the country to hesitate in choosing?

Among the plainest signs of the times in America is the popular distrust of legislators. The citizens are gradually and surely resuming the law-making and money-spending power unwisely delegated in the past to bodies whose custom it is to abuse the trust. "Government" has come to mean a body of representatives with interests as often as not opposed to those of the great mass of electors. Were legislation direct, the circle of its functions would speedily be narrowed; certainly they would never pass legitimate bounds at the urgency of a class interested in enlarging its own powers and in increasing the volume of public outlay. Were legislation direct, the sphere of every citizen would be enlarged; each would consequently acquire education in his rôle, and develop a lively interest in the public affairs in part under his own management.

And what so-called public business can be right in principle, or expedient in policy, on which the American voter may not pass in person? To reject his authority in politics is to compel him to abdicate his sovereignty. That done, the door is open to pillage of the treasury, to bribery of the representative, and to endless interference with the liberties of the individual.

THE WAY OPEN TO PEACEFUL REVOLUTION.

What I set out in the first chapter to do seems to me done. I essayed to show how the political "machine," its "ring," "boss," and "heeler," might be abolished, and how, consequently, the American plutocracy might be destroyed, and government simplified and contracted to the field of its natural operations. These ends achieved, a social revolution would be accomplished—a revolution without loss of a single life or destruction of a dollar's worth of property.

Whoever has read the foregoing chapters has seen these facts established :

(1) That much in proportion as the whole body of citizens take upon themselves the direction of public affairs, the possibilities for political and social parasitism disappear. The "machine" becomes without effective uses, the trade of the politician is rendered undesirable, and the privileges of the monopolist are withdrawn.

(2) That through the fundamental principles of democracy in practice—the Initiative and the Referendum—great bodies of people, with the agency of central committees, may formulate all necessary law and direct its execution.

(3) That the difference between a representative government and a democracy is radical. The differ-

ence lies in the location of the sovereignty of society.
The citizens who assign the lawmaking power to officials surrender in a body their collective sovereignty.
That sovereignty is then habitually employed by the
lawgivers to their own advantage and to that of a twin
governing class, the rich, and to the detriment of the
citizenship in general and especially the poor. But
when the sovereignty rests permanently with the citizenship, there evolves a government differing essen-
tially from representative government. It is that of
mere stewardship and the regulation indispensable to
society.

The Social Forces Ready for Our Methods.

Now that our theory of social reform is fully sub-
stantiated by fact, our methods shown to be in harmony with popular sentiment, our idea of democratic
government clearly defined, and our final aim political
justice, there remains some consideration of early
possible practical steps in line with these principles
and of the probable trend of events afterward.

Having practical work in view, we may first take
some account of the principal social forces which may
be rallied in support of our methods :— .

To begin with : Sincere men who have abandoned
hope of legislative reform may be called to renewed
effort. Many such men have come to regard politics
as inseparable from corruption. They have witnessed
the tediousness and unprofitableness of seeking relief
through legislators, and time and again have they seen

the very officials elected to bring about reforms go
over to the powers that exploit the masses. They have
seen in the course of time the tricks of partisan legislators almost invariably win as against the wishes of
the masses. They know that in politics there is little
study of the public needs, but merely a practice of the
ignoble arts of the professional politician. Here, however, the proposed social reorganization depends, not
on representatives, but on the citizens themselves;
and the means by which the citizens may fully carry
out their purposes have been developed. A fact, too, of
prime importance: Where heretofore in many localities the people have temporarily overthrown politician
and plutocrat, only to be themselves defeated in the
end, every point gained by the masses in direct legislation may be held permanently.

Further: Repeatedly, of late years, new parties have
risen to demand justice in government and improvement in the economic situation. One such movement
defeated but makes way for another. Proof, this, that
the spirit of true reform is virile and the heart of the
nation pure. The progress made, in numbers and
organization, before the seeds of decay were sown in
the United Labor party, the Union Labor party, the
Greenback-Labor party, the People's party of 1884, and
various third-party movements, testify to the readi-
ness of earnest thousands to respond, even on the slight-
est promise of victory, to the call for radical reform.
That in such movements the masses are incorruptible
is shown in the fact that in every instance one of the

chief causes of failure has been doubt in the integrity of leaders given to machine methods. But in direct legislation, machine leaders profit nothing for themselves, hold no reins of party, can sell no votes, and can command no rewards for workers.

Again : The vast organizations of the Knights of Labor and the trades-unions in the American Federation of Labor are evidence of the willingness and ability of wage-earners to cope practically with national problems. And at this point is to be observed a fact of capital significance to advocates of pure democracy. Whereas, in independent political movements, sooner or later a footing has been obtained by a machine, resulting in disintegration, in the trades organization, while political methods may occasionally corrupt leaders, the politician labor leader uniformly finds his fellow workmen turning their backs on him. The organized workers not only distrust the politician but detest political chicanery. Such would equally be the case did the wage-workers carry into the political field the direct power they exert in their unions. And in politics this never-failing, incorruptible power of the whole mass of organized wage-workers may be exerted by direct legislation. Therewith may be had politics without politicians. As direct legislation advances, the machine must retire.

Here, then, with immediate results in prospect from political action, lies encouragement of the highest degree—alike to the organized workers, to the men grown hopeless of political reform, and to the men in active rebellion against the two great machine ridden parties.

Encouragement founded on reason is an inestimable practical result. Here, not only may rational hope for true reform be inspired ; a lively certainty, based on ascertained fact, may be felt. All men of experience who have read these pages will have seen confirmed something of their own observations in direct legislation, and will have accepted as plainly logical sequences the developments of the institution in Switzerland. The New Englander will have learned how the purifying principles of his town meeting have been made capable of extension. The member of a labor organization will have observed how the simple democracy of his union or assembly may be transferred to the State. The "local optionist" will have recognized, working in broader and more varied fields, a well tried and satisfactory instrument. The college man will have recalled the fact that wherever has gone the Greek letter fraternity, there, in each society as a whole, and in each chapter with respect to every special act, have gone the Initiative and the Referendum. And every member of any body of equal associates must perceive that the first, natural circumstance to the continued existence of that body in its integrity must be that each individual may propose a measure and that the majority may accept or reject it ; and this is the simple principle of direct legislation. Moreover, any mature man, east or west, in any locality, may recall how within his experience a com-

munity's vote has satisfactorily put vexatious questions at rest. With the recognition of every such fact,
hope will rise and faith in the proposed methods be
made more firm.

Abolition of the Lawmaking Monopoly.

To radical reformers further encouragement must
come with continued reflection on the importance to
them of direct legislation. In general, such reformers
have failed to recognize that, before any project of
social reconstruction can be followed out to the end,
there stands a question antecedent to every other.
It is the abolition of the lawmaking monopoly. Until that monopoly is ended, no law favorable to the
masses can be secure. Direct legislation would de-
stroy this parent of monopolies. It gone, then would
follow the chiefer evils of governmental mechanism—
class rule, ring rule, extravagance, jobbery, nepotism,
the spoils system, every jot of the professional trading
politician's influence. To effect these ends, all schools
of political reformers might unite. For immediate
purposes, help might come even from that host of conservatives who believe all will be well if officials are
honest. Direct majority rule attained, inviting opportunities for radical work would soon lie open. How,
may readily be seen.

The New England town collects its own taxes; it
manages its local schools, roads, bridges, police, public
lighting and water supply. In similar affairs the Swiss
commune is autonomous. On the Pacific coast a ten-

dency is to accord to places of 10,000 or 20,000 inhabitants their own charters. Throughout the country, in many instances, towns and counties settle for themselves questions of prohibition, license, and assessments; questions of help to corporations and of local public improvement. Thus in measure as the Referendum comes into play does the circumscription practicing it become a complete community. In other words, with direct legislation rises local self-government.

The Principles of Local Self-Government.

From even the conservative point of view, local self-government has many advantages. In this country, the glaring evils of the State, especially those forming obstacles to political improvement and social progress, come down from sources above the people. Under the existing centralization whole communities may protest against governmental abuses, be practically a unit in opposition to them, and yet be hopelessly subject to them. Such centralization is despotism. It forms as well the opportunity for the demagogue of to-day—for him who as suppliant for votes is a wheedler and as politician and lawgiver a trickster. Centralization confuses the voter, baffles the honest newspaper, foments partisanship, and cheats the masses of their will. On the other hand, to the extent that local independence is acquired, a democratic community minimizes every such evil. In naturally guarding itself against external interference, it seeks in its connection with other communities the least common political bonds. It is watchful of the home rule principle. Under its local self-government, government plainly becomes no more than the management of what are wholly public interests. The justice of lopping off from government all matters not the common affairs of the citizens then becomes apparent. The character of every man in the community being known, public duties are intrusted with men who truly represent the citizens. The mere demagogue is soon well known. Bribery becomes treachery to one's neighbor. The folly of partisanship is seen. Public issues, usually relating to but local matters, are for the most part plain questions. The press, no longer absorbed in vague, far-off politics, aids, not the politicians, but the citizens. Reasons, every one of these, for even the conservative to aid in establishing local self-government.

But the radical, looking further than the conservative, will see far greater opportunities. In local self-government with direct legislation, every possibility for his success that hope can suggest may be perceived. If not in one locality, then in another, whatever political projects are attainable within such limits by his school of philosophy may be converted by him and his co-workers from theory to fact. Thence on, if his philosophy is practicable, the field should naturally widen.

The political philosophy I would urge on my fellow-citizens is summed up in the neglected fundamental principle of this republic: Freedom and equal rights.

The true point of view from which to see the need of the application of this principle is from the position of the unemployed, propertyless wage-worker. How local self-government and direct legislation might promptly invest this slave of society with his primary rights, and pave the way for further rights, may, step by step, be traced.

The Relation of Wages to Political Conditions.

The wages scale pivots on the strike. The employer's order for a reduction is his strike ; to be effective, a reserve of the unemployed must be at his command. The wage-worker's demand for an increase is his strike ; to be effective it must be backed up by the indispensableness of his services to the employer. Accordingly as the worker forces up the scale of wages, he is the more free, independent, and gainer of his product. To show the most direct way to the conditions in which workers may command steady work and raise their wages, this book is written. For the wages question equitably settled, the foundation for every remaining social reform is laid.

To-day, in the United States, in scores, nay, hundreds, of industrial communities the wage-working class is in the majority. The wage-workers commonly believe, what is true, that they are the victims of injustice. As yet, however, no project for restoring their rights has been successful. All the radical means suggested have been beyond their reach. But in so far as a single community may exercise equal rights

and self-government, through these means it may
approximate to just social arrangements.

Any American city of 50,000 inhabitants may be
taken as illustrative of all American industrial communities. In such a city, the economical and political
conditions are typical. The immediate commercial
interests of the buyers of labor, the employers, are
opposed to those of the sellers of labor, the employed.
To control the price of labor, each of these parties in
the labor market resorts to whatever measures it finds
within command. The employers in many branches
of industry actually, and employers in general tacitly,
combine against the labor organizations. On the
wage-workers' side, these organizations are the sole
means, except a few well-nigh futile laws, yet developed to raise wages and shorten the work day. In
case of a strike, the employers, to assist the police in
intimidating the strikers, may engage a force of armed
so-called detectives. Simply, perhaps, for inviting
non-unionists to cease work, the strikers are subject to
imprisonment. Trial for conspiracy may follow arrest,
the judges allied by class interests with the employers.
The newspapers, careful not to offend advertisers,
and looking to the well-to-do for the mass of their
readers, may be inclined to exert an influence against
the strikers. The solidarity of the wage-workers in-
complete, even many of these may regard the fate of
the strikers with indifference. In such situation, a
strike of the wage-workers may be made to appear to

all except those closely concerned as an assault on the bulwarks of society.

But what are the bulwarks of society directly arrayed against striking wage-workers? They are a ring of employers, a ring of officials enforcing class law made by compliant representatives at the bidding of shrewd employers, and a ring of public sentiment makers— largely professional men whose hopes lie with wealthy patrons. Behind these outer barriers, and seldom affected by even widespread strikes, lies the citadel in which dwell the monopolists.

Such, in outline, are the intermingled political and economic conditions common to all American industrial centres. But above every other fact, one salient fact appears : On the wage-workers falls the burthen of class law. On what, then, depends the wiping out of such law? Certainly on nothing else so much as on the force of the wage-workers themselves. To deprive their opponents of unjust legal advantages, and to invest themselves with just rights of which they have been deprived, is a task, outside their labor organizations, to be accomplished mainly by the wage-workers. It is their task as citizens—their political task. With direct legislation and local self-government, it is, in considerable degree, a feasible, even an easy, task. The labor organizations might supply the framework for a political party, as was done in New York city in 1886. Then, as was the case in that campaign, when the labor party polled 68,000 votes, even non-unionists might throw in the reinforcement of their otherwise hurtful strength. Success once in sight, the organized wage-workers would surely find citizens of other classes helping to swell their vote. And in the straightforward politics of direct legisla- tion, the labor leaders who command the respect of their fellows might, without danger to their character and influence, go boldly to the front.

The Wage-Workers as a Political Majority.

Suppose that as far as possible our industrial city of 50,000 inhabitants should exercise self-government with direct legislation. Various classes seeking to reform common abuses, certain general reforms would immediately ensue. If the city should do what the Swiss have done, it would speedily rid its adminis- tration of unnecessary office-holders, reduce the salar- ies of its higher officials, and rescind outstanding franchise privileges. If the municipality should have power to determine its own methods of taxation, as is now in some respects the case in Massachusetts towns, and toward which end a movement has begun in New York, it would probably imitate the Swiss in progres- sively taxing the higher-priced real estate, inheri- tances, and incomes. If the wage-workers, a majority in a direct vote, should demand in all public work the short hour day, they would get it, perhaps, as in the Rockland town meeting, without question. Further, the wage-workers might vote anti-Pinkerton ordinances, compel during strikes the neutrality of the police, and place judges from their own ranks in at least the local courts. These tasks partly under way, a change in prevailing social ideas would pass over the community. The press, echo, not of the widest spread sentiments, but of controlling public opinion, would open its columns to the wage-working class come to power. And, as is ever so when the wage-workers are aggressive and probably may be dominant, the social question would burn.

The Entire Span of Equal Rights.

The social question uppermost, the wage-workers—now in political ascendency, and bent on getting the full product of their labor—would seek further to improve their vantage ground. Sooner or later they would inevitably make issue of the most urgent, the most persistent, economic evil, local as well as general, the inequality of rights in the land. They would affirm that, were the land of the community in use suitable to the general needs, the unemployed would find work and the total of production be largely increased. They would point to the vacant lots in and about the city, held on speculation, commonly in American cities covering a greater area than the land improved, and denounce so unjust a system of land tenure. They could demonstrate that the price of the land represented for the most part but the power of the owners to wring from the producers of the city, merely for space on which to live and work, a considerable portion of their product. They could with reason declare that the withholding from use of the vacant

land of the locality was the main cause of local poverty. And they would demand that legal advantages
in the local vacant lands should forthwith cease.

In bringing to an end the local land monopoly,
however, justice could be done the landholders. Un-
questionably the fairest measure to them, and at the
same time the most direct method of giving to city
producers, if not free access to land, the next practicable thing to it, would be for the municipality to con-
vert a part of the local vacant land into public property, and to open it in suitable plots to such citizens
as should become occupiers. Sufficient land for this
purpose might be acquired through eminent domain.
The purchase money could be forthcoming from several sources—from progressive taxation in the direct
forms already mentioned, from the city's income from
franchises, and from the savings over the wastes of
administration under present methods.

From the standpoint of equal rights there need be
no difficulty in meeting the arguments certain to be
brought against this proposed course—such sophistical
arguments as that it is not the business of a government to take property from some citizens to give to
others. If the unemployed, propertyless wage-worker
has a right to live, he has the right to sustain life. To
sustain life independently of other men's permission,
access to natural resources is essential. This primary
right being denied the wage-workers as a class, any or
all of whom, if unemployed, might soon be propertyless, they might in justice proceed to enforce it. To

enforce it by means involving so little friction as those here proposed ought to win, not opposition, but approval.

Equal rights once conceded as just, this reasoning cannot be refuted. Discussed in economic literature since before the day of Adam Smith, it has withstood every form of assault. If it has not been acted on in the Old World, it is because the wage-workers there, ignorant and in general deprived of the right to vote, have been helpless; and if not in the New, because, first, until within recent years the free western lands, attracting the unemployed and helping to maintain wages, in a measure gave labor access to nature, and, secondly, since the practical exhaustion of the free public domain the industrial wage-workers have not perceived how, through politics, to carry out their convictions on the land question.

Our reasoning is further strengthened by law and custom in state and nation. In nearly every state, the constitution declares that the original and ultimate ownership of the land lies with all its people; and hence the method of administering the land is at all times an open public question. As to the nation at large, its settled policy and long-continued custom support the principle that all citizens have inalienable rights in the land. Instead of selling the national domain in quantities to suit purchasers, the government has held it open free to agricultural laborers, literally millions of men being thus given access to the soil. Moreover, in thirty-seven of the forty-four states, execution for debt cannot entirely deprive a man of his homestead, the value exempt in many of the states being thousands of dollars. Thus the general welfare has dictated the building up and the securing of a home for every laboring citizen.

In line, then, with established American principles is the proposition for municipal lands. And if municipalities have extended to capitalists privileges of many kinds, even granting them gratis sites for manufactories, and for terms of years exempting such real estate from taxation, why not accord to the wage-workers at least their primary natural rights? If any property be exempted from taxation, why not the homesite below a certain fixed value? And if, for the public benefit, municipalities provide parks, museums, and libraries, why not give each producer a homesite—a footing on the earth? He who has not this is deprived of the first right to do that by which he must live, namely, labor.

Effects of Municipal Land.

A city public domain, open to citizen occupiers under just stipulations, would in several directions have far-reaching results.

Should this domain be occupied by, say, one thousand families of a population of 50,000, an immediate result, affecting the whole city, would be a fall in rents. In fact, the mere existence of the public domain, with a probability that his tenants would remove to it, might cause a landlord to reduce his rents.

Besides, the value of all land, in the city and about it, held on speculation, would fall. Save in instances of particular advantage, the price of unimproved residence lots would gravitate toward the cost, all things considered, of residence lots in the public domain. This, for these reasons : The corner in land would be broken. Home builders would pay a private owner no more for a .lot than the cost of a similar one in the public area. As houses went up on the public domain, the chances of landholders to sell to builders would be diminished. Sellers of land, besides competing with the public land, would then compete with increased activity with one another. Finally, just taxation of their land, valueless as a speculation, would oblige landowners to sell it or to put it to good use.

Even should the growth of the city be rapid, the value of land in private hands could in general advance but little, if at all. With the actual demands of an increased population, the public domain might from time to time be enlarged ; but not, it may reasonably be assumed, at a rate that would give rise to an upward tendency of prices in the face of the above-mentioned factors contributing to a downward tendency.

At this point it may be well to remember that, conditions of land purchase by the city being subject to the Referendum, the buying could hardly be accompanied by corrupt bargaining.

When the effect of the public land in depressing land values, in other words in enabling producers to retain the more of their product, was seen, private as

well as public agencies might aid in enlarging the
scope of that effect. The philanthropic might transfer
land to the municipality, preferring to help restore
just social conditions rather than to aid in charities
that leave the world with more poor than ever; the
city might provide for a gradual conversion, in the
course of time, of all the land within its limits to
public control, first selecting, with the end in view,
tracts of little market value, which, open to occupiers,
would assist in keeping down the value of lands held
privately.

But the more striking results of city public land
would lie in another direction. The spontaneous ef-
forts of each individual to increase and to secure the
product of his labor would turn the current of production away from the monopolists and toward the producers. With a lot in the public domain, a wage-worker
might soon live in his own cottage. As the settler
often did in the West, to acquire a home he might first
build two or four rooms as the rear, and, living in it,
with later savings put up the front. A house and a
vegetable garden, with the increased consequent thrift
rarely in such situation lacking, would add a large
fraction to his year's earnings. Pasture for a cow in
suburban city land would add yet more. Then would
this wage-earner, now his own landlord and in part a
direct producer from the soil, withdraw his children from the labor market, where they compete for
work perhaps with himself, and send them on to
school.

What would now happen should the wage-workers of the city demand higher wages? It is hardly to be supposed that any industrial centre could reach the stage of radical reform contemplated at this point much in advance of others. When the labor organizations throughout the country take hold of direct legislation, and taste of its successes, they will nowhere halt. They will no more hesitate than does a conquering army. Learning what has been done in Switzerland, they will go the lengths of the Swiss radicals and, with more elbow room, further. Hence, when in one industrial centre the governing workers should seek better terms, similar demands from fellow laborers, as able to enforce them, would be heard elsewhere.

The employer of our typical city, even now often unable to find outside the unions the unemployed labor he must have, would then, should he attempt it, to a certainty fail. The thrifty wage-working householder, today a tenant fearful of loss of work, could then strike and stay out. The situation would resemble that in the West twenty years ago, when open land made the laborer his own master and wages double what they are now. Wages, then, would perforce be moved upward, and hours be shortened, and a long step be made toward that state of things in which two employers offer work to one employé. And, legal and social forces no longer irresistibly opposed to the wage-workers, thenceforth wages would advance. At every stage they would tend to the maximum possible under the improved conditions. In the end, under fully equal

conditions, everywhere, for all classes, the producer
would gather to himself the full product of his labor.

The average business man, too, of the city of our
illustration, himself a producer—that is, a help to the
consumer—would under the better conditions reap new
opportunities. Far less than now would he fear failure
through bad debts and hard times ; through the wage-
workers' larger earnings, he would obtain a larger volume of trade ; he would otherwise naturally share in
the generally increased production ; and he would
participate in the common benefits from the better
local government.

But the disappearance of the local monopolist would
be predestined. The owner of local franchises would
already have gone. The local land monopolist would
have seen his land values diminished. In every such
case, the monopolist's loss would be the producer's
gain. The aggregate annual earnings of all the city's
producers (the wage-workers, the land-workers, and
the men in productive business) would rise toward
their natural just aggregate—all production. As between the various classes within the city, a condition
approximating to justice in political and economic arrangements would now prevail.

What would thus be likely to happen in our typical
city of 50,000 inhabitants would also, in greater or
less degree, be possible in all industrial towns and
cities. In every such place, self-government and direct legislation could solve the more pressing immediate phases of the labor question and create the local

conditions favorable to remodeling, and as far as possible abolishing, the superstructure of government.

Wider Applications of These Principles and Methods.

The political and economic arrangements extending beyond the control of the municipalities would now, if they had not done so before, challenge attention. In taking up with reform in this wider field, the industrial wage-workers would come in contact with those farmers who are demanding radical reforms in state and nation. As the sure instrument for the citizenship of a state, direct legislation could again with confidence be employed. No serious opposition, in fact or reason, could be brought against it. That the mass of voters might prove too unwieldy for the method would be an assertion to be instantly refuted by Swiss statistics. In Zurich, the most radically democratic canton of Switzerland, the people number 339,000 ; the voters, 80,000. In Berne, which has the obligatory Referendum, the population is 539,000. And it must not be overlooked that the entire Swiss Confederation, with 600,000 voters, now has both Initiative and Referendum. Hence, in any state of the Union, direct legislation on general affairs may be regarded as immediately practicable, while in many of the smaller states the obligatory Referendum may be applied to particulars. And even in the most populous states, when special legislation should be cast aside, and local legislation left to the localities affected, complete direct legislation need be no more unmanageable than in the smallest.

United farmers, wage-workers, and other classes of citizens, in the light of these facts, might naturally demand direct legislation. Foreseeing that in time such union will be inevitable, what more natural for the producing classes in revolt than to unite today in voting, if not for other propositions, at least for direct legislation and home rule? These forces combined in any state, it seems improbable that certain political and economic measures now supported by farmer and wage-worker alike could long fail to become law. Already, under the principle that "rights should be equal to all and special privileges be had by none," farmers' and wage-workers' parties are making the following demands: That taxation be not used to build up one interest or class at the expense of another; that the public revenues be no more than necessary for government expenditures; that the agencies of transportation and communication be operated at the lowest cost of service; that no privileges in banking be permitted; that woman have the vote wherever justice gives it to man; that no force of police, marshals, or militiamen not commissioned by their home authorities be permitted anywhere to be employed; that monopoly in every form be abolished and the personal rights of every individual respected. These demands are all in agreement with the spirit of freedom. Along the lines they mark out, the future successes of the radical social reformers will most probably come. But if, in response to a call nowadays frequently heard, the many incipient parties should decide to unite on one or a few things, is it not clear that in natural order the first reforms needed are direct legislation and local self-government?

To a party logically following the principle of equal rights, the progress in Switzerland under direct legislation would form an invaluable guide. The Swiss methods of controlling the railroads and banks of issue, and of operating the telegraph and telephone services, deserve study and, to the extent that our institutions admit, imitation. The organization of the Swiss State and its subdivisions is simple and natural. The success of their executive councils may in this country assist in raising up the power of the people as against one man power. The fact that the cantons have no senates and that a second chamber is an obstacle to direct legislation may here hasten the abolition of these nurseries of aristocracy.

With the advance of progress under direct legislation, attention would doubtless be attracted in the United States, as it has been in Switzerland, to the nicer shades of justice to minorities and to the broader fields of internal improvement. As in the cantons of Ticino and Neuchâtel, our legislative bodies might be opened to minority representatives. As in the Swiss Confederation, the great forests might be declared forever the inheritance of the nation. What public lands yet remain in each state might be withheld from private ownership except on occupancy and use, and

the area might be so increased as to enable every producer desiring it to exercise the natural right of free
access to the soil.   Then the right to labor, now being
demanded through the Initiative by the Swiss workingmen's party, might here be made an admitted fact.
And as is now also being done in Switzerland, the
public control might be extended to water powers and
similar resources of nature.

Thus in state and nation might practicable radical
reforms make their way.   From the beginning, as has
been seen, benefits would be widespread.   It might not
be long before the most crying social evils were at an
end.   Progressive taxation and abolition of monopoly
privileges would cause the great private fortunes of
the country to melt away, to add to the producers'
earnings.   On a part of the soil being made free of
access, the land-hungry would withdraw from the
cities, relieving the overstocked labor markets.   Poverty of the able-bodied willing to work might soon be
even more rare than in this country half a century
ago, since methods of production at that time were
comparatively primitive and the free land only in the
West.   If Switzerland, small in area, naturally a
poor country, and with a dense population, has gone
far toward banishing pauperism and plutocracy, what
wealth for all might not be reckoned in America, so fertile, so broad, so sparsely populated!

And thus the stages are before us in the course of
which the coming just society may gradually be
established—that society in which the individual shall

attain his highest liberty and development, and consequently his greatest happiness. As lovers of freedom even now foresee, in that perfect society each man will be master of himself ; each will act on his own initiative and control the full product of his toil. In that society, the producer's product will not, as now, be diminished by interest, unearned profits, or monopoly rent of natural resources. Interest will tend to disappear because the products of labor in the hands of every producer will be abundant—so abundant that, instead of a borrower paying interest for a loan, a lender may at times pay, as for an accommodation, for having his products preserved. Unearned profits will tend to disappear because, no monopolies being in private hands, and free industry promoting voluntary coöperation, few opportunities will exist for such profits. Monopoly rent will disappear because, the natural right to labor on the resources of nature made a legal right, no man will be able to exact from another a toll for leave to labor. Whatever rent may arise from differences in the qualities of natural resources will be made a community fund, perhaps to be substituted for taxes or to be divided among the producers.

The natural political bond in such a society is plain. Wherein he interferes with no other man, every individual possessing faculty will be regarded as his own supreme sovereign. Free, because land is free, when he joins a community he will enter into social relations with its citizens by contract. He will legislate (form contracts) with the rest of his immediate community in person, Every community, in all that relates peculiarly to itself, will be self-governing. Where one community shall have natural political bonds with another, or in any respect form with several others a greater community, the circumscription affected will legislate through central committees and a direct vote of the citizenship. Executives and other officials will be but stewards. In a society so constituted, communities that reject the elements of political success will languish ; free men will leave them. The communities that accept the elements of success, becoming examples through their prosperity, will be imitated ; and thus the momentum of progress will be increased. Communities free, state boundaries as now known will be wiped out ; and in the true light of rights in voting—the rights of associates in a contract to express their choice—few questions will affect wide territories. Rarely will any question be, in the sense the word is now used, national ; the ballot-box may never unite the citizens of the Atlantic coast with those of the Pacific. Yet, in this decomposition of the State into its natural units—in this resolving of society into its constituent elements—may be laid the sole true, natural, lasting basis of the universal republic, the primary principle of which can be no other thing than freedom.

INDEX.

Liberty

❧ NOT THE DAUGHTER BUT THE MOTHER OF ORDER ❧

PUBLISHED WEEKLY.

PIONEER ORGAN OF ANARCHISM IN AMERICA.

BENJ. R. TUCKER, EDITOR.

Two Dollars a Year.   Single Copies, Four Cents.

A thoughtful, resolute, unique, uncompromising, unterrified, consistent, severely critical, able, fair, and honest exponent of the doctrine that Equal Liberty is the necessary basis of Social Harmony.

A journal edited to suit its editor, not its readers. If it suits its readers, so much the better.

UNPARALLELED PREMIUMS.

Every person sending $2 for a year's subscription to LIBERTY enjoys the privilege, while the subscription continues, of *buying all books, periodicals, and stationery at wholesale prices.* In April, 1893,

One Subscriber Alone Saved $30.37

by this privilege; very many subscribers save over $10 a year by it; nearly every subscriber saves more than the cost of subscription. This is the *most valuable premium ever offered by a newspaper.*

Every *new* subscriber agreeing to send $2, and *mentioning this advertisement*, will receive LIBERTY for a year, together with the above-named privilege, and an outright gift of the following books: MY UNCLE BENJAMIN, by Tillier, paper, 312 pages, retailing at 50 cents; THE RAG-PICKER OF PARIS, by Pyat, illustrated, paper, 325 pages, retailing at 50 cents; CHURCH AND STATE, by Tolstoi, paper, 169 pages, retailing at 25 cents; THE FRUITS OF CULTURE, by Tolstoi, paper, 185 pages, retailing at 25 cents; A TALE OF TWO CITIES (Dickens's greatest novel) and SKETCHES BY BOZ, paper, retailing at 25 cents. These are not cheap books. The type is large and the paper good.

The subscriber, if he prefers, may select, instead of the six volumes just mentioned, the following: SHAKSPERE'S COMPLETE WORKS, one volume, royal octavo, bound in extra cloth and stamped in gold, and EMERSON'S ESSAYS, first and second series, two volumes, 12 mo, cloth, in a box.

Every *new* subscriber agreeing to send $4, and *mentioning this advertisement*, will receive LIBERTY for a year, the wholesale-price privilege, and a set of

THE COMPLETE WORKS OF CHARLES DICKENS,

in Fifteen Volumes of 400 to 500 pages each, *bound in cloth*, stamped in gold and black, large type, good paper, 237 illustrations.

The books in each case will be sent by express, the subscriber to pay expressage. No advance remittance required, for, if desired, the goods will be sent C. O. D. But the subscriber is advised to remit in advance, as he will thus have to pay the express company *only* for carriage, and *not* its charge for collecting the bill.

Send Subscriptions and Letters to

BENJ. R. TUCKER, 120 Liberty St. (top floor), NEW YORK CITY

SAFE POLITICS FOR LABOR.

"AMERICAN FEDERATION OF LABOR,
"NEW YORK, May 17, 1892.

"*Mr. J. W. Sullivan*:

"DEAR SIR:—I have had the extreme pleasure of reading your book, 'Direct Legislation,' and beg to assure you that it made a deep impression upon my mind. The principles of the Initiative and Referendum so often proclaimed find sufficient elucidation in concise form. The facts that you have massed together of the practical application of these principles give the best evidence of thorough research and study. It is the first time that the labor reformers and thinkers generally have had this subject presented to them in so able and readable a manner. Every man who believes in minimizing the evil tendencies of politics as a trade or profession, cannot fail to be highly interested as well as pleased upon reading your book.

"In many of the trade organizations the Initiative and the Referendum are applied, and I have no doubt in my mind whatever that with the growth and development of the trades-union movement, much will be done to apply the principles to our political government.

"I am led to believe that now in the New England states, particularly in Massachusetts, where the town meetings exert a large influence upon the public affairs of their respective localities, much could be done to bring the subject of the Initiative and Referendum to the attention of the masses. I think the trades-unionists of that section of the country would be more than willing to co-operate in an effort to demonstrate the practicability as well as the advisability of the adoption of that idea.

"Again assuring you of the pleasure I have had in perusing the work, and thanking you earnestly for your contribution toward the literature upon this important subject, I am fraternally yours,   SAMUEL GOMPERS,
President American Federation of Labor."

"What I abandon legislatures and politicians and caucuses and all the paraphernalia of elective and debating bodies? Well, not quite; still very much curtailing the functions of these bodies and making laws by the direct action of the people themselves and curtailing the interference of professed legislators . . . The little volume is worthy of study, if only to know how some communities get along without the trouble and contradiction involved in the systems of other popular constituencies."—*New York Commercial Advertiser.*

"Certainly the author is to be commended for contributing many facts to our political knowledge—not the least of which is that we are no more, as we were fifty years ago, leaders of the world in genuinely popular government—for simplicity of treatment, and a most direct and lucid way of pointing out the results of certain measures."—*Chicago Times.*

"The author is eminently qualified to describe the working of a law to which the attention of the electors of this continent is being largely directed."—*London (Canada) Daily Advertiser.*

"We would recommend the book to every one desirous of learning in brief terms just what the Referendum is all about, and what good it would do."—*New Nation.*

"The appearance of such a book is not without political significance, and Mr. Sullivan's collection of data is convenient to have."—
New York Evening Post.

"The author shows that in Switzerland there has been a growth away from the representative system toward a pure democracy."—*Christian Register.*

"The historic facts are stated with a clearness and conciseness that make them valuable."—*New York Press.*

"Shows plainly how the politican might be abolished."—*Chicago Express.*

"Plainly and well written, and should be widely read."—*Christian Patriot.*

"Its subject is of the highest importance to the country."—
Switchman's Journal.

"Few books have done, we believe, more good in this century."—Rev. W. D. P. Bliss.